BINGLEY

A LIVING HISTORY

ALAN CATTELL

First published 2016

Published by
Chris Thorpe Graphic Design Ltd
Office 9, Unit 18,
Calderdale Business Park,
Club Lane, Ovenden,
Halifax HX2 8DS
www.ct-graphicdesign.co.uk   www.bingleyhistoryseries.co.uk
© Alan Cattell, 2016

ISBN: 978-0-9956437-0-3

CONTENTS

FOREWORD BY NICK SALT

Saltaire and the life of Sir Titus Salt are an important part of my family history and over the years I have become particularly interested in the life and achievements of his youngest surviving son, my great-grandfather Titus Salt Jnr. When visiting the ruins of his extravagant mansion at Milner Field I have usually walked up on the old carriage road from Saltaire, past the South Lodge, and was only vaguely aware that the house and its extensive gardens and model farm were actually in Gilstead, on the outskirts of Bingley.

A later connection with the town was that both my parents worked for the BBC North Region, and in 1946 my father John Salt chose Bingley for the first broadcast of the Wilfred Pickles radio show 'Have A Go' from the Modern School (now Beckfoot). The show went on to be very successful and ran for the next 21 years.

Recently, as part of a weekend of History Walks, I was taken on a fascinating circular walk around Bingley by Alan Cattell. This included visiting the Bingley 3 and 5 Rise Locks, Gawthorpe Hall, Oakwood Hall, Bingley Teacher Training College, The Mechanics Institute, The Butter Cross, Stocks and Market Hall and the Parish Church. I had not before fully realised the historic scope of the town and its surrounding area. During this walk Alan outlined the changes, particularly in governance and law which began to affect Bingley from 1847 onwards. In many ways these paralleled the changing fortunes of the Salt family during the same period. The history of Milner Field, and the background to 'Have A Go' were researched and covered by Alan in his first book *Bingley and Surrounds – Forgotten Moments from History* (2011).

Later the same day we walked along the canal bank, stopping briefly at the Fishermans Inn and over Scourer Bridge, then up Primrose Lane to Milner Field Farm. Both this farm, owned by Titus Salt Jnr., and Ferniehurst Farm at Baildon, owned by his elder brother Edward Salt,

Alan and Nick Salt at Milner Field Farm, May, 2016.

were built as Model Farms to mirror the Model Village approach taken at Saltaire. Alan's research has also shown that four of Sir Titus Salt's sons were involved in farming in some form, and that his own father Daniel Salt had also been a farmer for a while before moving into the Bradford woollen industry.

As an architectural consultant I have always had a great interest in buildings and their history, especially in West Yorkshire. My recent visit to Bingley has confirmed the wealth of historic buildings and institutions that the town still has, and the wish by residents to preserve these. Linked to this, governance of the town continues to evolve and change as witnessed by the creation of a new Town Council in 2016. Alan's new book *Bingley - A Living History* is a testament to his wish on behalf of others to capture change while it is happening, recording memories before they are lost forever.

Nick Salt - Mid Wales. September 2016

FOREWORD BY JAMIE ROBERTS

Ever since I was young I've always been fascinated by the notion of bringing history to life. Whilst it will always be important to write down and record significant memories and events, to me the challenge is to keep the essence of them alive.

As the great great grandson of Sir James Roberts I have been fortunate to be able to play an active part in preserving the family heritage and our links to industrial Yorkshire. Knowing the strong family connection with alpacas and their wool, I brought three of them to the Kilnsey Estate in 2013. Their names are Titus, Bertie and Silver – after the three men who were such defining influences upon the history of Saltaire. I walked them through the streets of the town dressed as Sir James, to commemorate the one hundred and twentieth anniversary of my great great grandfather taking over Salts Mill from the family of the founder Titus Salt.

The success of the mill enabled my family to purchase the Kilnsey Estate in 1911 and it has remained in the family since then. Bringing alpacas home to Kilnsey was a fantastic way of celebrating my family's heritage and connections with Salts Mill, and bringing the story to life for the tens of thousands of visitors we get each year.

It's thanks to the dedicated work of researchers such as Alan Cattell that we have recently been able to add more detail and colour to the lives and events of the past. It was on a walk to the ruined mansion of Milner Field – once lived in by my family – that Alan mentioned in passing that trout had been reared and farmed there by my great great grandfather. My own father had established a trout farm at Kilnsey in 1978, either an extraordinary coincidence or proof that the apple never falls far from the tree!

Fresh discoveries are being made all the time. I recently found out that Edward Salt was a member of the prestigious Kilnsey Angling Club for many years. Edward Salt was one of Sir Titus Salt's sons and lived at Ferniehurst in Baildon. The connection between the Salt family and Kilnsey may in turn provide a connection with how the Roberts family found out about the Kilnsey Estate and subsequently purchased it.

Alan Cattell has also brought to light that both families had strong links to farming. In the 1870s Titus Salt Jr and Edward Salt set up Model Farms on their estates. It was fascinating to discover that one of my relatives Harry Roberts, son of Sir James, also set up a very successful Model Farm at his estate on Jersey in the 1920s. These are covered in the chapter on Milner Field Farm on page 84.

This book represents a proactive approach to capturing living history by engaging people in exploring their own family history. As someone who is already doing this myself, I fully recommend this approach in helping you to establish your own links to the past.

Jamie Roberts, Kilnsey Estate, September 2016

Alan and Jamie Roberts at the Salt Building, Saltaire.

PREFACE

Then

My previous book *"Bingley and Surrounds - Forgotten Moments from History"* outlined the building up of the road, canal and rail infrastructure in Bingley and the change from agriculture to industrialisation and transition from village to town. The main aspects of governance in this period were the Lord of the Manor and the Vestry.

This new book is intended to capture the further changes in governance brought about by the Bingley Improvement Commissioners (1847) and Bingley Urban District Council (1894). They were responsible for building up further infrastructure in the town to include gas, electricity and sanitation provision, plus other services to cater for a growing population.

Now

The one thing constant about change is change itself as will be shown in the Chronological Changes in Governance (page 40) Since 1984 Bradford Metropolitan Council has been the main body of influence for Bingley and surrounds. Recent years have seen the demise of many buildings and institutions in Bingley brought about by economic necessity, technology or world change.

Current Bingley residents are equally as proud of their local history as their forebears as is evidenced by the number of voluntary friends' associations. These include Friends of Bingley College, Bingley Swimming Pool, Prince of Wales Park and St Ives, all of which were founded to remember and preserve in some part much loved institutions/buildings.

Other institutions and buildings no longer exist. The Bradford and Bingley Building Society, built in 1962, was demolished in 2015 leaving empty space where the "top of town" and Myrtle Place existed many years ago. Some of the Main Street pubs identified by Elizabeth Downsborough in her two books on Bingley Pubs have changed their names - The Fleece to the Potting Shed, The Queens Head to the Bingley Ale House and The Midland to Maverick's. The Conservative

Club, built in 1913, has now become Martinez Wine Shop and Wine Bar.

Local artist Jane Fielder, whose Gallery at 29, Park Road displays many paintings known locally as "Janescapes", is a resident who is interested in presenting the changing face of Bingley through her art. She has been successful with her quirky urban landscapes in depicting Bingley in a humorous and original manner. She says: *"On a bright day, I can look across the never ending rows of terraces with their chimneys casting black shadows, echoed by vast mill chimneys, highlighted only by rows of billowing washing and bras the size of windows, and think it is the most wonderful place in the world".*

Much of her work is intended to capture views of landscapes and buildings before they are lost. Jane has given permission for the image of Bingley which forms the front cover of this book, to be reproduced, as her contribution to living history. This work was painted as a celebration of the birth of her first grandchild, a more personal angle on the living history theme.

Living History

Part of my intention in writing this book has been to chronicle change that has happened (about which little is known or has been written) and to capture change that is currently happening, which may be of future historical interest. This living history approach includes interviews I have carried out with people who have been involved at first-hand with events or whose relatives have been involved. I believe that it is important that these are recorded before they become distant memories or are lost forever.

Acknowledgements

In addition to the invaluable support given by my family, a number of people have been significant in my research leading to the publication of this book. Among them are my friends Brian Billcliff and his nephew, Alex Homer, who have been critical readers. Julie Woodward at Shipley College, Saltaire Archives and staff at Bradford Libraries (particularly at Bingley and Keighley) and Sue Caton (now retired) who have given advice and access to research materials and photographs. Members of the Bingley and District Local History Society have given access to their archives and photographs including those of Stanley Varo. They and Derek Gott at Cullingworth Local History Group who have given support, encouragement and a platform for sharing interest in local history. Bingley 5 Rise Frocks W.I have also given a regular platform. Invaluable access to postcards and photographs has been provided by the Graham Hall Archives, Mick Walmsley, of Woodbank Nurseries, Harden, The Friends of Bingley College, the late Graham Carey, staff at Bingley Swimming Pool, the Downs Family at Milner Field Farm and Doreen Thompson. Jane Fielder has given copyright permission for one of her original paintings to be reproduced as the front cover to this book.

Additionally thanks go to Susan Brown, Stuart Clark, John Collins, David Downs, Stephen Duxbury, Geoff Hoyle, Arthur and Mary Pitchforth, Jamie Roberts, Nick Salt, Doreen Thompson, Barry Watson and Michael Wilde for sharing their own or their family history memories with me.

Grateful thanks are offered to readers of the now defunct local community magazine Bingley Hub for the regular feedback and encouragement they have given me over the past five years. Simon Harrup and Kimberley Devine Harrup, the editors also provided a springboard and encouragement for me to write my first book.

For his encouragement and design support in my writing and publishing this second book my enduring thanks go to Chris Thorpe of Chris Thorpe Graphic Design, Halifax. Chris was closely involved in the production of my first book and this experience has been invaluable in he and I learning from that experience and producing this second book.

If anyone has not been acknowledged this is the fault of the author as are any inadvertent errors in the text. If any copyright has been infringed apologies are offered as there has been no deliberate intent and every effort has been made to obtain permission, acknowledge and attribute content wherever possible.

Alan Cattell - Bingley. August 2016

INTRODUCTION

The book is divided into four sections, the content of which is summarised below:

Section One - Governance including Chronological Time Lines - Change

This section identifies the different stages of Governance as Bingley developed from an agricultural base into an industrial manufacturing town. The Chronological Time Line tracks the changes in Governance that have happened over the period 1847 to 2016 and latterly the influence of the Bingley Improvement Commissioners, Bingley Urban District Council and Bradford Metropolitan District Council.

From April 2016 certain aspects of Community Governance returned to the local area under the auspices of Bingley Town Council covering Bingley, Cottingley, Crossflatts, Eldwick, Gilstead and Micklethwaite.

Section Two - Photographs of Bingley Town Centre Capturing the Changes

Section Two provides a pictorial record and brief narrative of the development of some of the main buildings and thoroughfares in Bingley. Many of these were as a result of changes in Governance within the town, specifically around Main Street, Old Main Street, Longbottom's Smithy, Park Road, Central Bingley, Chapel Lane, Top of Town and Myrtle Place.

Section Three - Places and People
Places

In this section significant additions to the town in the late 1800s and early 1900s are identified. A narrative chapter on each will be detailed in this section.

Myrtle Park

While the Prince of Wales Park had been opened some way from the town centre in 1865, it was not until 1908 that **Myrtle Park** was opened, close to the town's main facilities. In 2016 it still exists as a well utilised public park and venue for events such as Bingley Show and Bingley Music Live.

Bingley Fire Station

The first purpose built **Fire Station** was built in Market Street in 1902 and remained there until the 1973 when it moved to Keighley Road, Bingley. This chapter covers the development of the **Fire Brigade** and the purchase of fire fighting equipment in Bingley.

Milner Field Farm

My previous book *Bingley and Surrounds - Forgotten Moments from History (2011:84)* included coverage of the commissioning and building of Milner Field Mansion and estate for Titus Salt Junior. By 1902 the Milner Field Estate had changed ownership from the Salt family to the Roberts family. As a result, the tenancy of **Milner Field Farm** also changed and the Downs family became the new tenants, a tenancy which the family still holds in 2016. This chapter captures that change and also chronicles the original building of a **model farm** which matched the model village approach that Titus Salt had taken in building Saltaire.

Bingley Teacher Training College for Women

Up to 1905, many female teachers had become so through on-the-job experience as untrained Pupil Teachers. In 1909, as a result of a national initiative, the West Riding County Council chose Bingley to build **Bingley Teacher Training College for Women**. The College was opened in 1911 until it closed in 1978. The main college building and several of the residential student halls are now flats and apartments, while two have become Residential Care Homes.

Bingley Cinema's

Cinema came to Bingley with the **Hippodrome** being built in 1913 on land previously occupied by Longbottom's Smithy. The site of the cinema is now a public car park. In 1921, the **Myrtle Cinema** was opened on the site now occupied by Wetherspoons Myrtle Grove Public House, which still retains many of the building features of the original cinema.

Bingley Swimming Pool

Bingley's first **public baths** opened in 1892 providing access to bathing facilities which previously only the rich could afford. The first **swimming baths** including the **Princess Hall** were opened in 1927. This chapter covers their opening and subsequent development.

Events and People

In this section I have attempted to give a flavour of the times and of changing attitudes by identifying **people** and **events** which **demonstrate change.** Some could be termed "old school" recognition of national events/people organised by Bingley Urban District Council.

Others highlight the efforts of union members and the Suffragettes to gain recognition for their causes. Three significant people born and raised in Bingley are also identified, namely, an entrepreneur who grew his local business into an instantly recognisable national company; a second who became an acclaimed national and international stage and screen character actress; and the third a renowned academic, writer and broadcaster who essentially educated himself. Again, a narrative chapter on each will be detailed in this section.

Events
Queen Victoria's Jubilee Celebrations in Bingley

Two major Jubilee Celebrations were held in Bingley, one to celebrate Queen Victoria's Golden Jubilee in 1887 and the other, her Diamond Jubilee in 1897. The latter essentially heralded the end of an era. As the start of the new century commenced, change in the old order in Bingley was already beginning to happen. Queen Victoria died in January 1901 at the age of 81, after nearly 64 years as Queen.

Milner Field Drowning Tragedy

In 1902 the Postmans Federation (formed in 1895) held an event at **Milner Field Pond** on the Milner Field Estate at Gilstead. Unfortunately, during the event the local Branch Secretary **drowned**. The event had been organised to raise funds for the **Bradford Postmans Federation strike fund** - an early indication of union militancy.

Boer War Commemoration in Bingley

Bingley Urban District Council organised an event in 1905 at which a church service was organised at Bingley Parish Church to commemorate **Bingley** men killed in the **Second Boer War in South Africa (1899 - 1902)**. General Rundle, one of the commanding officers of the campaign presented medals to local men who had fought in the war at the then **Town Hall** at the **Mechanics Institute** (now Library Taps pub) on Main Street.

A Sufragette in Bingley

In 1907 the **Suffragette Movement** organised a protest march on the Houses of Parliament. During my research at Keighley Library into another topic I discovered a letter in the Keighley News to the **women of Bingley** from **Nell Kenney**, one of the imprisoned suffragettes. This chapter traces her history and her connection with Bingley and also her contribution to a large suffragette rally at **Shipley Glen** in 1908.

General Booth in Bingley

In 1907 a Civic Presentation was organised by **Bingley Urban District Council** to welcome **General Booth,** the founder of the **Salvation Army**, to **Bingley**. This chapter describes his brief visit to the town.

People
Magnet Joinery

In the early 1900s the Duxbury family owned a greengrocer's shop in Mornington Road, Bingley. In 1906 one of the sons, Tom is rumoured to have traded his horse named **Magnet** and sold the greengrocer's in exchange for a firelighter business thus named **Magnet Firelighters.** This chapter follows his progress as a local entrepreneur in growing his business, originally on Whitley Street, Bingley into one of the UK's largest kitchen and joinery manufacturers by the time that he died in 1948.

From Mill Owners Daughter to Stage and Screen Actress

George Henry Aked owned and ran Airedale Mills in Micklethwaite and later became a member of Bingley Urban District Council. His daughter, **Muriel Aked,** was active in local amateur dramatics in Bingley prior to attending and appearing at Liverpool Repertory Company in 1916 and later touring the Far East as an actress. From 1922 until she retired in 1953, she became a renowned **theatre** and **screen actress,** acting with some of the most famous theatre and film stars in the UK. This chapter follows her career.

Fred Hoyle

Fred Hoyle, born in Gilstead in 1915, was, among other notable achievements, an Academic, Mathematician, Astrophysicist Astronomer, Cosmologist, Broadcaster and Science Fiction Writer who coined the phrase Big Bang Theory then rejected it in favour of Steady State Theory. Controversial and forthright, he was known throughout his career for his independence of mind and as a lifelong rebel eager for intellectual combat. He was Knighted in 1972. This chapter traces his unique approach to learning while growing up in Bingley and includes comment by his son, Geoff, who has shared some of his recollections with me.

Section Four - Living History

The final section of the book is the result of interviews I have carried out locally to research the histories of families who were either born in Bingley area or have come from further afield to live here. These include:

Sue Brown, nee Green, whose great great grandfather was the first Town Crier and Pinder appointed in Bingley in 1853, a tradition carried out by the same family up until 1954.

Stuart Clark, who carried out research into his family tracing them back to 1651 and who established that his ancestors had never moved more than a mile from the same part of Bingley where they were born, in over 300 years.

Doreen Thompson, now living in Bingley whose mother, Doris Evelyn Reeve, born in Barnoldswick, attended Bingley Teacher Training College as a student between 1926 and 1928 and who recounted her time at the college and her joy at having trained in such a beautiful location.

Michael Wild, from the USA, who visited Bingley in 2014 and whose family left Bingley in 1907 to settle in America. Michaels' ancestry includes William Wild, one of the stonemasons who built the Five Rise Locks in 1773/74. Michael is also a relative of Lily Elstub (nee Seller) who worked in Bingley as a telephonist and also as landlady/barmaid at the Old Queens Head. Lily was the aunt of Peter Sellers, the renowned comedian and film star. She was the sister of Peter Sellers' father, Bill (orginally born William Seller).

Barry Watson, of Crossflatts, who was a notable long distance endurance swimmer in the 1960s and set a world record for swimming the English Channel from France in 1964. This record was not broken until 1981. In this chapter, Barry shares his memories of a momentous period in his life.

SECTION ONE
HISTORICAL GOVERNANCE AND LAW IN BINGLEY

Introduction

There have been a number of distinct phases of change in Governance in Bingley but it is less easy to establish exact dates in the transition from one to another. This is because political and socio-economic changes happen over different periods of time when the old is not necessarily immediately replaced by the new.

This chapter seeks to identify major changes and track their progress in chronological order and to be illustrative rather than exhaustive in approach. Neither is the chapter intended to replicate what has already been covered by notable local historians such as Dodd, Speight and Horsfall-Turner. Where they have identified and detailed particularly the influences of the Church and Lords of the Manor up to the 18th Century, I will, after brief links back to that period and those influences, concentrate on the period from the 19th Century up to 2016.

To do so I will also identify significant landowners whose presence shaped the development of Bingley as well as cataloguing the bodies and events which shaped Governance to the present day. These include the Bingley Improvement Commissioners (1847 - 1894), Bingley Urban District Council (1894 - 1974) and Bradford Metropolitan Council (1974 to date).

My intention is to capture key historical events and milestones in the development of governance and infrastructure in Bingley as a town, not to identify or discuss the political persuasions of those involved.

Attempting to guide my readers through a maze of sometimes complex, conflicting or not always chronological events and facts has been challenging, especially when trying not to miss out important detail. I would ask you in reading this chapter to be patient in gaining knowledge of Bingley's sometimes complicated governance. I can fully appreciate why no-one else has tried to attempt this previously!

Lords of the Manor

There have been eight Barons/Lords of Bingley, the first being Gospatric circa 1070 and the last George Lane Fox who held the title from 1933 until he died in 1947, with no further issue.

Each Lord of the Manor of Bingley up until the 18th Century would have "governed" his Manor within the infrastructure described below:

Manor Courts

In feudal society in medieval times, the Lord of the Manor took responsibility for the government of the local community. **Manor Courts** were run which exerted administrative control over such matters as land succession within the manor, but also functioned as a local court of law for routine offences.

In effect the Manor Courts were the lowest courts of law in England during the feudal period. They had a civil jurisdiction which was limited both in what they could do and in terms of geography. They dealt with matters over which the Lord of the Manor had jurisdiction, (primarily torts, local contracts and land tenure) and their powers only extended to people who lived within the lands of the manor.

Court Baron and Court Leet

Manor Courts were of two types, one the **Court Baron** and the other, the **Court Leet** both of which existed in Bingley.

The Court Baron administered the customs of the Manor and dealt with offences against it.

The Court Leet was responsible for maintaining freeman's oaths of peacekeeping and good practice in trade. It also enforced law and order through trial by jury to ensure the punishment of small crimes and petty offences. The court also dealt with the nomination and appointment of local officials such as constables. Such courts latterly ensured that sales of food, drink and agriculture were adhered to. On a number of occasions the Court Baron and Court Leet would meet together on the same day for ease of administration.

Each had separate jurisdiction, governing distinct areas of life in the manor. However, the boundaries of jurisdiction blurred over the years and often one court sitting would deal with matters previously dealt with by the separate courts. Eventually, with the growth in influence of local magistrates/justices of the peace and the growing power of the church authorities, the Court Leet fell into decline and had all but died out by the 19th Century.

Court of Requests

The Court Baron previously held at Kings Head in Bingley for the recovery of small debts was extended by Act of Parliament in 1777. This established a **Court of Requests** for the recovery of debts under 40 shillings. It amassed enough money to build its own courthouse in Myrtle Place (1831).

A significant reform in 1846 was the Small Debts Act which abolished the old Courts of Requests that dealt with civil matters and replaced them with a new network of some 500 County Courts throughout England and Wales.

As a result, the Court of Requests moved from Bingley to Keighley and became a County Court in 1847.

Magistrates Courts/ Petty Sessions

In the 19th Century the passing of sentences and punishment for summary and minor crimes at local level were carried out by Justices of the Peace/Magistrates.

Those appointed as JPs/Magistrates were usually prominent citizens and landowners whose social position and economic power meant that their authority was difficult to question. In Bingley William Busfeild Ferrand, of St Ives, and William Ellis, of Castlefields, were two such magistrates.

Local Bingley Courts were generally held in public houses, namely the White Horse, Brown Cow and Ferrands. Crimes such as gambling, poaching and drunkenness, petty theft, default of fine payments, public affray and disorder were heard and sentences passed or referred to a higher court.

Brown Cow.

As regards jail, courthouse and police facilities notable dates for the building of or transfer of facilities and responsibilities were:

1821 New lock up built next to Workhouse in Myrtle Place

1860 New Courthouse and Police Station built at County expense in Myrtle Place

1929 New Court House and Police Station built on Bradford Road

2011 Court House closed and powers transferred to Keighley

2012 Keighley Magistrates and County Courts closed. Cases moved to Bradford or Skipton

Significant Local Landowners

In making comment about the Lane Fox family being Lords of the Manor, White (1837:677) observed that much land, however, was owned by Edward Ferrand Esq, of St Ives, and two other significant landowners, namely William Busfeild Senior and Junior and Walker Ferrand.

The Ferrands and the Busfeilds because of their position in owning substantial land in the area had significant influence in Bingley and surrounds.

The Ferrand family had originally purchased Harden Grange in 1636 and the Busfeild family had bought Ryshworth Hall in 1672. Marriages between the two families had taken place, the first being when the widowed Anne Busfeild had married Robert Ferrand in 1686. In later years the Busfeilds owned Myrtle Grove in Bingley and the Ferrands owned Harden Grange and St Ives.

William Busfeild Ferrand

William Busfeild Ferrand particularly exerted influence over the local area in the 1840s and 1850s both as a local magistrate and through his links with Benjamin Disraeli and the Young England Party. He was considered by many to be the local squire because of his considerable ownership of land.

He had been born William Busfeild but assumed the name and arms of the Ferrand family in 1839 after the death of his uncle, Edward Ferrand, without issue in 1837. As Member of Parliament for Knaresborough from 1841 to 1847, Ferrand was actively involved in sponsoring the Ten Hours Factory Act and had helped expose the harsh conditions of the way in which Poor Law was administered.

He had also been in sympathy with the Young England movement whose leaders, including Disraeli and Lord John Manners wanted to revive an enlightened form of feudalism where the upper classes as a form of "squirearchy" fulfilled their duty of responsibility for the well being of the "lower orders" and in return, gaining their loyalty. Disraeli and Manners visited Bingley in 1844 and stayed with Ferrand, part of the reason being to espouse the Young England cause locally.

William Busfeild Ferrand.

Despite his brave ideals, his role as a magistrate in what was called the Little Siege of Bingley in 1848 brought him into direct conflict with the Chartist movement in Bingley. This in addition to his tough stance as a magistrate when dealing with poachers resulted in him getting a very mixed press locally.

Finally, as the role of the Bingley Improvement Commissioners developed from 1847 onwards, the relationship between Ferrand and the Commissioners (many of whom were Bingley millowners and manufacturers), became increasingly strained.

Burnley (1875:20) captures the tensions around these "politics of progress" in a republished article in the Charles Dickens sponsored magazine publication *All the Year Round*.

"Bingley – Four parallel lines intersect the valley. One of these is the main street, a second is the river which is spanned by a triple arched bridge, the third is the railway and the fourth is the great Leviathan canal. The canal and river belong essentially to the past: the main street has an eye to past, present and future; but the railway seems to point to the future alone.

From the side of the valley which is bordered by the river, there rise a succession of fertile woods, like "cloud on cloud" and in a green expanse beyond there stands the ancestral mansion of the Squire of the parish.

On the opposite hillside that slopes up to a purple ridge of moorland, the green of the pastures and meadows is dotted with palatial residences of merchant princes and manufacturers.

Thus, the representatives of the old and new confront each other, and try to stare each other out of countenance; the one backed up by a sense of prestige which is the outcome of high birth, and the other by a feeling of superiority engendered by the knowledge that wealth can even outbuy the advantages of birth and station.

There is no love lost between the two orders of men.

The Squire manages to enlist under his banner all the remnants of ancient gentility which have survived in the neighbourhood, while the money making seigniors command the sympathies of the migratory hordes who have found their way to the town to assist the great steam god in his work of filling the world with new garments".

While attempting to put a humorous slant on the situation, Burnley captures the essence of the tensions arising.

Writing a year later, Cudworth (1876:192) observes: *"The present Lord of the Manor is Mr George Lane Fox, yet the real "squire" of the parish is Mr William Ferrand who is deputy-lieutenant of the West Riding and chairman of the Bingley and Keighley Petty Sessional Division and whose mansion is situated on the plateau overlooking the road from Bingley to Harden".*

This identifies the strategic politician in Ferrand, who had actively sought and gained higher office in the West Riding and a position of authority above that of local magistrate, within the wider legal framework of the area.

William Busfeild Ferrand died in March 1889.

Alfred Sharp

Harrison (1997:7) observed that during this period, Alfred Sharp in particular was a principal benefactor to the town and people of Bingley. She identified that in 1861 he had made a substantial contribution towards the cost of the Wesleyan Day School and that in 1874 he and his brother had subscribed about £6,000 towards the building of the new Wesleyan Methodist Church on Mornington Road.

Harrison states: *"Again when the new Technical Institute was built in 1889, Alfred Sharp made a handsome contribution. He was, it seemed taking over work for the town performed by Squire Ferrand. When Squire Ferrand died in 1889, Alfred Sharp was already giving verbal support to the building of a Public Library in the Mechanics Institute. This was followed by material support of £1,000 towards the cost of necessary alterations and furnishings. Not only was the Mechanics Institute transformed into a Public Library but also into a Town Hall for Bingley.*

Mr Sharp had recently gone to reside at Myrtle Grove, having bought the estate from Squire Ferrand in 1874 for £13,500. In view of all these facts it is scarcely surprising that the townspeople were not averse to having their interests supported by a prominent mill owner rather than a hereditary land owner. All knew where Mr Sharp "made his brass". Apart from their first astonishment that a businessman should act with such generosity towards them, many deemed it "only right and proper" that money the townsfolk had helped to "make" should benefit the town".

Alfred Sharp died in June, 1896.

Alfred Sharp.

Church Influence and Vestry Meetings

As already identified previously, division of land into ancient parishes was linked to the manorial system: Parishes and manors often covered the same area and had the same boundaries. The manor was the principal unit of local administration and justice in the early rural economy.

During the course of the 16th and 17th centuries the power and activity of manorial courts in England and Wales, except in the leasing and transfer of manorial land, faded away.

Progressively the **church replaced** the **manor court** as the administrative centre. Many of the manor court functions were taken over by regular public meetings of clergy, churchwardens and parishioners which for generations had been held in the vestries of parish churches. The parish authorities thus became known as vestries.

Previously vestry meetings had been held to decide on questions and solutions relating to the possessions and fabric of the church. In the 16th century these vestry meetings were made increasingly responsible for minor law and order offences, the appointment of constables and the maintenance of the poor of the parish. The latter became a major aspect of vestry activity and, after the dissolution of the monasteries, the power to levy a rate to fund relief of the poor was conferred on the parish authorities by the Act for the Relief of the Poor 1601.

Vestry Meetings

Originally the "vestry" had raised money for the maintenance of the parish church by taxing householders and landowners through the church rate. As a result of the 1601 Act it was given power to levy taxes to maintain the poor (the poor rate).

Examples of vestry decisions in Bingley were essentially concerned with the upkeep of the church and relief of the poor. However the examples shown below in chronological order identify that other matters were also dealt with:

1726 A house in Myrtle Place was converted by Vestry into Bingley Workhouse

1776 Vestry set up a Standing Committee to act as Guardians of the Poor

1837 The Keighley Union was formed in 1837, under the New Poor Law 1834 which including Bingley-with-Micklethwaite

The vestry retained much of its importance until 1834 when with the removal for the majority of its responsibilities for the poor it gradually lost much of its power to the Bingley Improvement Commissioners and Local Government Board.

1856 Appointment of parish constables

1860 The Workhouse was transferred to Keighley

1862 The Vicar and Churchwardens distributed £30 to the ancient poor of the parish

April 30th, 1863 A public meeting of the Vestry was held in Bingley Parish Church to take into consideration the propriety of adopting the Local Government Act of 1858 for Bingley, Harden and Micklethwaite (except for the parts situated within the limits of the Bingley Improvement Act)

1868 The right to collect a church rate was abolished

1869 A Burial Board was elected by Vestry

1871 A new cemetery was opened

1875 A Vestry meeting decided to reduce the qualification of Improvement Commissioners to £5 as regards house ownership

1894 The Local Government Act transferred the remaining civil functions to elect parish and rural district councils

Bingley Improvement Commissioners 1847 - 1894

Boards of Improvement commissioners were *ad hoc* urban local government boards created during the 18th and 19th centuries. Around 300 boards were created in the United Kingdom, each by a private Act of Parliament, typically termed an Improvement Act. Gradually they replaced the older urban government forms such as the Lord of the Manor and Vestry which were ill-equipped to deal with the larger populations of the Industrial Revolution.

Accordingly, in 1844 a letter was sent to Bingley residents to discuss and give information on the Bingley Improvement Act.

As a result of the Bingley Improvement Act 1847 a number of Bingley residents and property owners connected with the town met at the Queens Head for the purpose of improving the lighting, paving, cleansing, sewerage, and draining of the streets in the town and neighbourhood of Bingley. They also looked at "matters of public concern" such as erecting of stalls in the market, public house hours of opening and licensing of hackney carriages.

These unpaid Bingley Improvement Commissioners included 41 local property owners who were to be replaced annually by election. Originally they were formed as an association of property owners for the joint improvement of their property and in that role it was agreed that they should have certain public rights and responsibilities. They were generally made responsible for regulating and improving the town in a supervisory capacity. Maps of the time show a defined Bingley Improvement Act district which represented a small fraction of the town. This district was extended in 1867.

In 1848 a Board of Health was formed as a result of the Public Health Act 1848. The Improvement Commissioners eventually responded in 1855 by appointing an Inspector of Nuisances and a Sanitary Inspector whilst also having a watching brief for tanneries, slaughterhouses, piggeries and stagnant pools.

1850 The Commissioners purchased a fire engine and were responsible for appointing a fire brigade

1853 The Commissioners introduced standards for cellar dwellings

1854 The Commissioners discussed the need for sewerage schemes and plans

1862 The Commissioners leased local waterworks and springs from their owners for a period of 30 years

1866 The Press were admitted to Bingley Improvement Commissioners meetings

1867 The Commissioners bought out the privately owned gasworks in Bingley for £2,600

Between 1865 and 1878 there was considerable construction of new housing in the area and much of the development was within the Improvement District around Park Road, Charles Street, Mornington Road, Clyde Street and Whitley Street. In 1876 it was recorded that 46 new streets had been laid out in the previous 12 years. New Mills and Churches were also built in the area which was termed to be "New Bingley". The Improvement Commissioners were involved in sanctioning plans for this building and ensuring that drains, pavements and roads were fit for purpose.

1871 The Commissioners introduced regulations for new buildings and guidelines for paving and draining of streets in new developments. These also stipulated that there must be on privy for every two houses

1890 The Commissioners leased the Mechanics Institute as a Town Hall and two years later converted the old news room into a Council Chamber

1890 Ratepayers adopted the Free Libraries Act. The building was also converted to hold a public baths in the basement

A major contribution to the library which opened in 1892 was made by local benefactor Alfred Sharp

1890 Bingley Cottage Hospital opened and was mainly supported by public subscriptions

Bingley Cottage Hospital.

Credit should be given to these unpaid members of the public who were instrumental in working for the improvement of the town. Their meetings eventually resulted in far reaching changes for the town.

Local Government Board 1863 - 1894

Commencing in 1863, while the Improvement Commissioners governed the town of Bingley within the boundaries defined within the Bingley Improvement Act, a Local Board was responsible for the what were termed the Outer Districts of Bingley. The Local Government Act Amendment Act of 1863 was regarded as a Sanitary law which addressed the need to supply adequate sanitation and clean water to the Outer Districts.

An announcement in the Bradford Observer on October 1st, 1863, stated

*"On Saturday last at the Court House, Bingley the first election took place of a Local Government Board for the District of the Township of Bingley which comprises the whole of Bingley **except** the portion of the town of*

Bingley situate within the limits of the Bingley Improvement Act".

Sanitary Laws were later replaced by the Public Health Act 1875 which designated local government districts as urban sanitary districts with the local board becoming the urban sanitary authority. The titles of the district and board did not change, however, the local board assuming extra duties as a sanitary authority.

Records show that in Bingley in May, 1889, the board undertook detailed discussion on the provision of and facilities for the treatment of sewage.

During 1894 local boards and local government districts were finally abolished by the Local Government Act 1894, when all urban sanitary districts became amalgamated with urban districts. A new Bingley Urban District Council was to govern the district within newly designated boundaries.

County Councils

County councils were created by the Local Government Act 1888, largely taking over the administrative functions of the unelected county courts of quarter sessions. County councils consisted of councillors, directly elected by the electorate and county aldermen, chosen by the council itself.

The West Riding County Council (WRCC) was the county council of the West Riding of Yorkshire from April 1st, 1889 to March 31st, 1974. The council met at County Hall in Wakefield.

The new system, established in 1889, was a major modernisation, which reflected the increasing range of functions carried out by local government in late Victorian Britain. A major accretion of powers took place when education was added to county council responsibilities in 1902. County councils were responsible for more strategic services in a region, with (from 1894) smaller Urban District Councils and Rural District Councils responsible for other activities.

Bingley Urban District Council 1894

The Local Government Act 1894 reformed local government and

followed the reforms carried out at county level in 1888. It introduced elected councils at district and parish level. As a result, Bingley Improvement Commissioners ceased to exist.

An urban district was a type of local government district that covered an urbanised area. Urban districts had an elected urban district council (UDC), which shared local government responsibilities with a county council.

Early Examples of Bingley UDC Activity

1894 Elections for a new Bingley Urban District Council were held. The new district was divided into seven wards

1895 The Local Board was replaced by Bingley Outer Urban District Council

1898 Amalgamation of the Urban Districts of Bingley, Bingley Outer and Wilsden

1900 Street lighting was improved

1902 The new Bingley UDC built a fire station on Elm Tree Hill

1907 Mechanics Institute and Technical School vested in the UDC

1908 Myrtle Grove estate was bought by the UDC

Further examples of activity are shown in the Chronological Timeline of Events with Governance Implications on page 40. The Timeline traces all governance activity from 1847 to 2016 and is particularly useful in identifying the significant advances made by Bingley Urban District Council between 1894 and 1974.

Below are examples of the main committees of Bingley UDC in 1936 and the types of office held by individuals. These are intended to demonstrate the scope of development of the by then well established UDC, and areas of responsibility.

At this time the local population was 21,540. There were 20 members of the UDC covering seven wards including Cullingworth and Wilsden and one representative of the UDC on the County Council.

Main Committees

- Lighting and Tramways
- Education and Libraries
- Parks and Allotments
- Transport and Fire Brigade
- Water and Baths
- Health, Maternity and Child Welfare
- Highways and Buildings
- Finance and General Purposes
- Housing. Rating and Valuation Sub-Committee
- Golf Course Sub-Committee

Officers

- Clerk and Solicitor
- Treasurer and Accountant - Rating and Valuation Officer
- Medical Officer of Health
- Health Visitor and School Nurse
- Engineer and Surveyor
- Architect
- Gas Engineer
- Electrical Engineer
- Baths Superintendant
- Sanitary Inspector
- Water Manager
- Manager of Sewage Disposal Works and Inspector of Trade Wastes
- Fire Brigade Superintendant
- Librarian
- Head Master, Technical and Evening Institutes

Bradford Metropolitan District Council 1974 - to date

In 1974, City Of Bradford Metropolitan District Council was created to administer the newly-formed metropolitan borough. The county borough of Bradford was merged with the Borough of Keighley, the Urban Districts of Baildon, Bingley, Cullingworth, Denholme, Ilkley, Shipley and Silsden, along with part of Queensbury and Shelf Urban District and part of Skipton Rural District by the Local Government Act 1972.

The responsibilities of Bradford MDC now cover:

- Education
- Highways
- Social Care
- Housing
- Libraries
- Cemeteries
- Leisure and Recreation
- Environmental Health
- Waste Collection and Disposal
- Planning Applications and Building Control
- Local Tax Collection
- Strategic Planning

Links with West Yorkshire

Bradford Metropolitan Council is one of the five metropolitan boroughs which make up the County of West Yorkshire. The others are Calderdale, Kirklees, Leeds and Wakefield.

West Yorkshire County Council was abolished in 1986 and so its districts (the metropolitan boroughs such as Bradford) effectively became unitary authorities.

However, this left the county without a single authority covering the whole area, although some council functions including Archive Services and Trading Standards continue to be provided jointly, through **West Yorkshire Joint Services** (created in 1997).

The **West Yorkshire Passenger Transport Executive** and **West Yorkshire Police** continue to operate across the county. The **West Yorkshire Fire and Rescue Service** is the county wide, statutory emergency fire and rescue service for West Yorkshire. It is administered by a joint authority appointed annually from across the five metropolitan boroughs of West Yorkshire and is known as the Fire and Rescue Authority.

Since April 1st, 2014, West Yorkshire has been a combined authority area, with the local authorities pooling together some functions covering strategic transport, economic development, and regeneration, as the **West Yorkshire Combined Authority**.

Arising from the restructuring described above there are now **three** levels of local government, namely **Combined Authorities** such as West Yorkshire, **Principal Authorities** such as Bradford and the potential for local **Parish/Town Authorities.**

Bingley Town Council (2016)
National Framework Background

In 2006 the Government established a Department for Communities and Local Government which was intended among other things to *"give more power to local people to shape what happens in their local area".*

2011 saw the introduction of a Localism Act to facilitate the devolution of decision-making powers from central government control to individuals, communities and local councils.

Both of the above were intended to recognise that Town/ Parish Councils are the first level of local government in the provision of community governance which underpins and supports local communities.

A Parliamentary Briefing Paper of May, 2015, however advised caution in what could be expected of a Town/Parish Council: *"Parish and Town Council powers are generally concurrent with (i.e. equivalent to) those of district councils. In practice, most lack the capacity to undertake provision of public services and concern themselves with local **environmental, community and amenity issues.***

Application in Bingley

The campaign for a local council in Bingley gained momentum in 2013 when it was backed by local voluntary organisations including Bingley Civic Trust, the town's Rotary Clubs and village societies and associations. Due to the dedicated effort of a group of individuals comprising the Bingley Community Council Group, the formation of a new Town Council was agreed by City of Bradford Metropolitan District Council in October, 2015.

The new Bingley Town Council serves Bingley, Cottingley, Crossflatts, Eldwick, Gilstead and Micklethwaite.

The Town Council became a formal body on April 1st, 2016. The first elections for new Town Councillors took place alongside the Bradford Council run elections on May 5th, 2016. Once the Town Councillors were elected the Town Council formally commenced putting in place its administrative duties and activities, independently to Bradford Council.

What the Town Council Can Do:

- Must be consulted about planning applications by Bradford MDC - planning, housing/town planning?
- Create neighbourhood plans and support local groups
- Develop tourism and regeneration strategies and deliver them
- Institute health and wellbeing initiatives
- Run public assets e.g toilets, allotments
- Organise community transport schemes
- Fund Christmas lights
- Take on or manage markets
- Establish community energy schemes

What the Town Council Can't Do:

- Take on responsibilities of a Principal Authority such as Education, Transport, Social Services, Development and Building Control or Environmental Health

Chapter Conclusion

In concluding this chapter and in line with my Living History approach, involving someone who was part of the decision making process in the period leading up to the transfer of governance to Bradford MDC in 1974, would seem appropriate. John G. Collins was the last Deputy Chairman between 1970 and 1974 in the final days of Bingley Urban District Council. The following comment by him represents his thoughts and views of both then and now: *"Basic democracy and representation in the Bingley of 1974 compared with the town's governance in mid – 2016 presents a much diluted recipe".*

Last Full Term of Bingley UDC

His memories are of 20 councillors, most, of whom were elected, who each "staunchly" represented the interests of the seven villages and central Bingley.

He recalls the 1970 elections: *"In each ward candidates had strong local support which meant that the democratic process reached well down into the roots of society. Once the 1970 election was over, the councillors, all living in the UDC and knowledgeable of its characteristics and needs, cooperated to fashion the best interests of Bingley as a whole".*

He also recalls that a number of major issues were confronted and dealt with at that time on behalf of the town without the need to trade off opportunities with other districts. He feels that the latter became a feature of the larger authority which replaced the UDC in 1974 and where other political and multi-cultural issues would become paramount.

Major Initiatives

One major works was the extension of the HQ of Bradford and Bingley Building Society which stood partly on Bingley UDC land abutting Myrtle Place. Some councillors regarded the building as being grotesque or too dominating. However it was appreciated that the building society was a major employer in the town, with the building being designed by a firm of local architects, thus bringing jobs and prosperity to the town.

Major works requiring significant funding were also undertaken with Yorkshire Water to improve the Dowley Gap sewage works. During this time the council looked after 49 miles of district roads, plus more than 2,000 council dwellings, the swimming pool, the allotments and cemeteries and the golf course at St Ives.

John recalls: *"One of the most memorable actions occurred in 1973 when Bingley UDC voted to use its remaining balances to build what was then known as the Arts Centre, thus using the funds for Bingley. The new building with quite revolutionary seati ng was built to connect to the existing St John's Ambulance building to form a new facility, with the Green Room for Bingley Little Theatre".*

2016.

Focus on Bingley

With the focus being firmly on Bingley, John notes that:

"With all this responsibility and detailed local involvement, the councillors were supported by a team of very capable and experienced senior officers all of whom along with their colleagues were employed by Bingley and dedicated their working time to the citizens of Bingley".

Not Within the Remit

He also observes that certain major issues were not within the remit of the UDC and that these included education, major highway matters, public utility provision, policing and fire brigade services.

Contrasts with 2016

In contrasting the governance situation between the Bingley UDC last term and 2016, John highlights the difficult job that the current three Metropolitan District Councillors (out of a total of 90 sitting at City Hall, Bradford) have.

His concern is that however good these councillors may be, in the face of diminishing funding for council initiatives and vociferous demands from other districts in the Metropolitan District Council, the needs of communities such as Bingley have been subsumed by other issues.

Though he applauds the major benefit to the town of the relief road, he voices concern over the possible demise of the swimming pool, Myrtle Place hardly being used, the vast undeveloped plot of waste land in the centre of Bingley where the building society once stood, the Courthouse having been closed and the still derelict cattle market and auction site, among a number of issues.

In reviewing present governance John highlights what he thinks is: *"A lack of a coordinated approach to achieve the best results for the citizens of Bingley as the town has become completely subsumed by the large and unwieldy size and structure that is Bradford Metropolitan District Council.*

Once known as "The Throstle Nest of Old England" Bingley, with the birth of the new Bingley Town Council, despite appearing to have limited powers, could still have a chance to "awake" as captioned Longfellow in his famous poem.

It will be very difficult to break free from Bradford, if not impossible, but if there is a desire to maintain the town's identity and enough Bingley folk with the energy and determination to fight this cause, I say "Good Luck "to them.

A CHRONOLOGICAL TABLE OF GOVERNANCE AND CHANGE

Year	Event
1847	**Constitution of the First Bingley Improvement Commission**
1847	Railway from Shipley to Keighley and Bingley railway station opened
1848	Bingley Gas Company formed (private)
1860	Workhouse transferred to Keighley
1860	New Courthouse and Police Station built at County expense in Myrtle Place
1863	First sod for Prince of Wales Park cut on wedding day of Prince of Wales
1864	Harden Road reservoir completed
1864	Mechanics Institute opened
1865	Voluntary labour/public subscription towards opening of Prince of Wales Park
1867	Gasworks purchased by Commissioners
1868	Market (Saturday) transferred to Myrtle Place
1868	Discontinuance of Tolls on the Keighley and Bradford Turnpike Road
1869	Prince of Wales Park acquired by Commissioners
1870	Bingley Burial Board formed
1871	New Sewerage Scheme
1872	Purchase of first steam Fire Engine
1881	Lease of water from St Ives estate
1881	Bingley Water and Improvement Act passed
1882	Market rights purchased from Lord of the Manor

1887 Bingley Technical School erected

1887 Central Cooperative Building opened on Main Street

1888 Old Market Hall, Butter Cross and Stocks removed to Prince of Wales Park

1888 Elm Tree Hill removed for widening of Main Street

1889 Bingley Technical School opened

1889 **West Riding County Council instituted**

1890 Mechanics Institute leased as Bingley Town Hall

1891 Bingley Cottage Hospital opened - supported by public subscription

Bingley Cottage Hospital.

1892 Mechanics Institute reading room converted into Council Chamber

1892 Opening of Public Library and Baths in Mechanics Institute

1892 New Bingley railway station opened

1894 **Improvement Commissioners reconstituted as Bingley Urban District Council**

1895 First Sewage Disposal works opened at Dowley Gap

1898 Urban Districts of Bingley, Bingley Outer and Wilsden amalgamated

1900 Bingley Sewerage and Sewage Disposal Works constructed

1900 Bingley Urban District Council Act passed

1901 Fire Station erected in Market Street

1903 New road (Keighley Road) made through Parish churchyard

1907 Mechanics Institute and Technical School vested in Bingley UDC

1908 Myrtle Park purchased

1911 Bingley Training College for Women Teachers opened by WRCC

1913 Bingley Tramway opened

1913 Bandstand built in Myrtle Park

1914 New Post Office erected in Main Street

1921 Bowling Green and three Tennis Courts built in Myrtle Park

1923 Bingley Education Week held

1924 Second Bowling Green at Myrtle Park

1926 Mechanics Institute handed over to Library

1926 Myrtle Grove became the Town Hall

1927 Princess Hall and Swimming Baths opened

1928 Mini Golf Course and Refreshment Pavilion - Myrtle Park

1928 St Ives Estate purchased from the Executors of the Ferrand Estate for £39,000

1929 Sports Turf Research Institute established at St Ives

1929 New Court House and Police Station

1931 St Ives Golf Course opened

1932 Electricity Offices on Main Street opened

1936 Town Planning Scheme approved

1936 Children's Paddling Pool - Myrtle Park

1937 Extensions to Princess Hall and Swimming Baths

1942 Bingley Modern and Technical School Opened

1945 Gift of land from Hempel Bros (Bingley) to extend Myrtle Park

1947 Wilsden Housing site purchased

1947 Cullingworth Housing site purchased

1948 Fire Brigade taken over by West Riding County Council

1948 Ambulance Service taken over by West Riding County Council

1948 National Health Service established

1948 Nationalisation of Electricity undertaking

1949 Nationalisation of Gas undertaking

1949 Formation of Bingley St Ives Municipal Golf Club

1949 Cottingley Housing Site purchased

1950 Bingley UDC proposes By-Pass (Relief Road)

1950 New bridge over the river at Myrtle Park

1953 Opening of a new sewage works at Dowley Gap

1954 Bingley Burial Board abolished and Bingley Cemetery vested in Bingley UDC

1956 York Street area acquired

1962 Opening of Ashfield Court and Myrtle Court

1962 Bingley Building Society Head Office opened

1962 Mobile Library services inaugurated

1964 Trunk Sewer Improvement Scheme adopted at a cost of £500,000

1967 Central area redevelopment scheme approved

1967 Traffic lights at Main Street/Park Road junction installed

1968 Multi storey flats at Crossley Wood opened

1969 Footbridge over the river at Cottingley Bridge

1970 2,000th Council House completed

1970 Major redevelopment of Central area of Bingley around Myrtle Grove, Chapel Lane, Main Street and 7 Dials area

1972 Trunk Sewer Improvement Scheme completed

1972 Myrtle Walk Shopping Centre opened

1973 Library at Mechanics Institute closed and moved to Shopping Centre

1973 New Library opened in Myrtle Walk Shopping Centre

1974 Bingley becomes part of Bradford Metropolitan District

1974 West Yorkshire CC replaced West Riding CC

1974 Bingley Arts Centre built and opened

1974 Old Holy Trinity church demolished

1975 Dedication of new Holy Trinity church

1979 Bingley Training College closed

1981 Maple Court opened

1984 Bingley Civic Trust raises funds to move the Butter Cross, Market and Stocks from Prince of Wales Park back to the centre of Bingley

1984 Bingley Civic Trust hand the restored Butter Cross, Market and Stocks back to Bradford MDC

1986 Metropolitan County Councils were abolished with most of their functions being devolved to the individual boroughs, making them de facto unitary authorities

1990 Bingley (St Ives) Golf Club privatised (on long-term lease with Bradford MDC)

1991 Better Bingley Campaign

1991 Music at Myrtle introduced

1992 Canal drained and diverted under Park Road bridge to make way for new Relief Road

1993 New canal bed completed

1994 New Park Road Bridge opened

1997 West Yorkshire Joint Services created

1998 Pulse Party in the Park (Partnership with Bradford MDC)

2002 Mornington Road Methodist Church demolished

2002 Bingley Technical School closed

2003 Bingley Relief Road (the new A650) opened

2003 New Mornington Road Methodist Church built and opened

2003 Friends of St Ives founded

2007 Bingley Music Live introduced

2008 New Children's Adventure Playground in Myrtle Park

2008 Myrtle Walk Shopping Precinct demolished

2009 Friends of Bingley College Reunion

2009 New Skate Park in Myrtle Park

2009 5 Rise Shopping Centre opened, replacing Myrtle Walk

2010 Bradford and Bingley Offices closed

2010 Canalside Medical Centre opened

2011 Bingley Hospital demolished

2011 New Beckfoot School built, the old one demolished

2011 Bingley Court Buildings closed

2012 Post (Sorting) Office Closed

2012 Bingley Arts Centre leased by Bingley Little Theatre from Bradford MDC

2013 Friends of Prince of Wales Park founded

2013 Bingley Council Shop closed down

2013 Proposal to close Swimming Pool

2013 Bingley Conservative Club for sale

2014 Pizza Hut closed and building merged with old Co-op shop and opened as Sainsbury's Local

2014 **West Yorkshire Combined Authority created**

2014 Yorkshire Bank closed

2014 Future of Town Hall?

2014 Reduction in Public Toilet opening times

2015 Friends of Bingley Swimming Pool became a Registered Charity

2015 HSBC Bank closed

2015 New Aldi Store opened

2015 Demolition of Bradford and Bingley building

2016 **Bingley Town Council became a formal body on April 1st**

2016 **Bingley Town Council Elections**

SECTION TWO

Photographs of Bingley town centre capturing the changes

While Section One highlighted the issues of governance in Bingley, Section Two presents a pictorial record capturing the changes to some notable landmarks (some brought about by governance initiatives) in the main town centre from 1880 to the present day.

MAIN STREET

This chapter shows the development of Main Street looking down from the junction of Main Street and Park Road towards the old Queens Head pub (now Bingley Ale House) and The Fleece (now the Potting Shed).

The year 1888 saw the removal of the Market Hall, Butter Cross and Stocks to the Prince of Wales Park and the demolition of Elm Tree Hill to enable Main Street to be widened to allow safer passage for pedestrians and horse drawn traffic.

The photographs show the transition to a wider, tree lined thoroughfare which included The Midland Hotel built in 1891 (now Maverick's) and the new Post Office (1914). They also show the changes in modes of transport and increase in different forms of traffic on Main Street.

Mechanised Transport

The first mechanised public transport, the tram, arrived in Bingley in 1913. Car and lorry transport developed from this period onwards. The route through the town centre was converted to public trolley buses in 1939 and the tram rails were removed during the Second World War. The trolley bus service was replaced by motor buses in November, 1963.

The anticipated rise in car ownership from the 1950s onwards led to Bingley Urban District Council proposing a by-pass as early as that date. However, it would take until 2003 before the relief road was eventually opened to relieve congestion in the town.

1894 Midland Hotel.

1896 Main Street.

1897.

1898.

1908.

1912.

1913 Bingley Tramway opening.

1930s.

1930s Main Street.

1935.

1940s.

1950s.

1980s.

1990s.

OLD MAIN STREET

This chapter shows the development of the lower section of Main Street from The Fleece (now the Potting Shed) looking down towards the Old White Horse pub, Old Main Street, the Parish Church and Keighley Road.

Changes
The Strand

The Fleece (also at one time the Excise Office) stands at the bottom of Main Street in an area once known as the Strand. At one time the Strand Stores, (102 Main Street), owned by Thomas Hemmant, was one of the most popular groceries in the area, particularly for its selection of cheeses and Bingley Blend Tea.

Millgate

Millgate and the junction leading over Ireland Bridge towards Harden was previously signposted as the Halifax-Howarth Turnpike Road during the 1800s. Elizabeth Downsbrough in her book *Bingley's Historic Pubs* (2011:57) records that when a suggestion about the widening of the road leading to Ireland Bridge was made to the Bingley Improvement Commissioners, comment was made that *"The road could easily be widened if Mr Ferrand could only pull down the White Horse Inn, which would be no loss to the town"*.

Old Main Street

The Improvement Commissioners in proposing widening of Main Street in the 1880s had to take account of the dangerous state of Old Main Street, The Keighley News of September 3rd 1904 reported: *"Because of the building of the new road with a length of 270 yards*

1904 New Main Street/Old Main Street.

and a width of 30 yards and being perfectly straight, all the dangers of the old road with its dangerous curve past the church are avoided".

1895.

The New Road

The eventual building of the new road (which took nearly two years) was not without its problems, both physical and financial. The new route of the road required the removal of nearly 2,500 bodies from the church graveyard which necessitated the passing of a Local Act in 1901 to enable this to happen.

Additionally the eventual cost to Bingley Urban District Council was nearly £14,000, more than half of which was needed to buy or demolish properties on Old Main Street and to purchase a portion of the graveyard. The new road opened in 1904.

1896 Old Main Street.

1896 Main Street from White Horse.

1896.

1900.

1901.

1902 Junction with Millgate.

1903 Main Street near Church.

1903.

1910 Bingley New Road.

1911 Old Main Street and new road.

1920 Main Street.

LONGBOTTOM'S SMITHY

One of Bingley's iconic buildings in the 18th and 19th centuries was known as Longbottom's Smithy, where at least four generations of the Longbottom family operated as blacksmiths over a period of 250-plus years. It was sited opposite the Strand area on Main Street described on page 49.

Records from June, 1864, show that Robert and Lucy Longbottom and their family lived in the premises, which they rented as a house and shed from the owner, William Ferrand, at a rateable value of £5/10 shillings. Later records show the smithy being rented from Mr Ferrand for £12 per year which was paid annually at the Brown Cow pub, where a free meal was provided.

In 1912 the smithy was demolished to make way for the first dedicated cinema in Bingley, the Hippodrome which opened in 1913. The history of cinema in Bingley and the eventual use of the site are covered on pages 106-111.

1894 Smithy.

1895 Lower Main Street.

1900 Smithy.

1910.

1911.

1912.

1913 Smithy, prior to demolition.

1915 Hippodrome Cinema.

1950s Hippodrome.

Woolworths, on old Hippodrome site.

2016 Car park on Woolworths site.

PARK ROAD

1900 Main Street and Park Road junction.

The bottom end of Park Road ends with a busy junction feeding on to Main Street, Bingley. It was previously called Toad Lane but renamed as Park Road because it was the thoroughfare leading to the newly opened Prince of Wales Park in 1865.

Toads and Frogs

Two bogs, the North and South bogs have been a feature of the Bingley landscape at the base of the valley since early times, and were home to thousands of toads. Speight (1898:250) in *Chronicles of Old Bingley* recalls that witnesses had told him *"Thousands of toads have been seen crossing the neck of land between the two mires. Park Road (up to 1863 when the first sod of the Prince of Wales Park was cut) had always been known for this reason as Toad Lane"*.

Changes in the Countryside

Hartley (1900:13) in *50 Years of Cooperation in Bingley* states: *"Bingley Town in 1850 may be said to have been located almost entirely on one side of the Leeds and Liverpool Canal. What is now Park Road was known by the not very euphonious name of Toad Lane, and was a somewhat narrow roadway, and a narrow side-walk on one side only.*

On the right in coming from the Main Street and nearly opposite the gates to the National School (now apartments) was a stile leading into fields, which was then a delightful path for a stroll all land bordering on Toad Lane on both sides was agricultural land. None of the houses now dotting the hillside were then built with the exception of Gawthorpe Hall, Beck House and the Old Vicarage".

Building

The change of name to Park Road in 1863 heralded the first of a number of occasions on which the road would be widened and improved. The main elements of building, from the corner of Main Street and leading up the steep hill occurred during a period starting in the early 1870s. By 1876 (206), Cudworth noted: *"The last 15 years have been very prolific in new buildings, but the greatest increase has taken place in the Park Road direction, or as it is now called "New Bingley". Here places of worship, huge mills and streets of houses have risen up as if by enchantment".*

Between 1889 and 1892 as a result of initiatives proposed by the Bingley Improvement Commissioners, Park Road was again widened.

1900 Looking up Park Road.

1903 Junction with Main Street.

1920 Looking down Park Road.

1930 Winter scene.

Photographs of Park Road

These are intended to show significant changes and views of Park Road from 1900 and then capturing views from 1920, 1930 and 1950. They also cover major improvements at the bottom end of Park Road during 1968 when road and bridge widening took place and 1969, 1980 and 1992 when Park Road bridge was rebuilt to facilitate rerouting of the canal because of Bingley Relief Road requirements.

1950 Park Road and Main Street junction.

1968 Road and bridge widening in Park Road.

1969 Fox's bakery, Park Road.

1969 Looking up Park Road.

1980 Park Road.

1992 Park Road bridge rebuild.

CENTRAL MAIN STREET

The area between Park Road and Chapel Lane became regarded as the central part of Main Street during the period 1864 and 1907. During that time the Mechanics Institute and Cooperative Central Stores were built on Main Street and featured in a number of Bingley's historical events of the time including Queen Victoria's Diamond Jubilee in 1897, the Boer War Commemoration of 1905 and General Booth's visit to the town in 1907.

Mechanics Institute

The Institute was opened in November, 1864, and since then, as covered in my previous book (74-77) has served the town as Town Hall, Public Baths, Library and nowadays as a public house, the Library Tap.

Cooperative Central Stores

These were built in 1887 and officially opened in April, 1888. While they are no longer used by the Co-op and are used by other enterprises, the facades and original shape of the buildings still exist.

1900 Mechanics Institute/Town Hall and Co-op building.

1900 Mechanics Institute/Town Hall and Co-op building.

1910 Looking towards Top of Town.

2016.

CHAPEL LANE

1880 *Chapel Lane from Myrtle Place.*

This chapter traces some of the events in the development of Chapel Lane which runs off Main Street.

These include the building of a Chapel which gave the lane its name, opening of shops by the early Co-operative movement in Bingley and trading by Rushton's Outfitters from the old chapel building.

Early Chapel

Victorian author William Cudworth (1876:203) in Round About Bradford (A Series of Sketches records: *"A meeting house was erected which is still standing, occupied as houses and shops in Chapel Lane. Of the precise year in which the old chapel was erected, there is no record".*

Building of Chapel and the first Minister

In fact there does appear to be a record. Dodd (1958:48) Bingley suggests that in 1694/95 Robert Walker *"built a chapel and lofted the same at his own charge, say for about £15".* Dodd also suggests that an existing chapel may have been converted.

The site of the chapel was on the corner of Main Street and Chapel Lane where the Post Office now stands. In 1695 noted clergyman Oliver Heywood presided at the foundation of the chapel (initially Presbyterian) with Accepted Lister as the first Minister. Speight (1895 :183) states: *"Here he preached in 1694 and finally settled in 1695, the house and the chapel being under the same roof"*.

Move of the Chapel - 1818

According to Horsfall-Turner (1897:159) the building in Chapel Lane, which by 1810 had been occupied for over 200 years, was *"incommodious and inadequate for the increased congregation"*. Consequently the old chapel became redundant and a new one was built at another site in Bingley and opened in 1818.

The Cooperative Movement in Bingley - 1850

A formative Cooperative Movement started in Bingley in the 1850s. Initially, Chapel Lane existed as a block of cottages, some of which were converted into shops were the Cooperative Society among others carried out business in its early years. The first Cooperative shop opened in Chapel Lane in 1854.

Over time between 1868 and 1874 further cottages were purchased which progressively became the Drapery, Central Grocery and Pork Departments. While the Cooperative opened a new Central Stores building in Main Street in 1888, Chapel Lane continued to be a much used site which also included Meeting Rooms.

Rushtons Outfitters

Rushtons were a popular Milliners, Hosiers, Shirt Makers, Costumiers and Drapers who occupied the old chapel building for many years. They also sold carpets, rugs, linoleum and blinds which catered for a fairly well-heeled clientele.

Baldwin (2005:42) records the observations of Henrietta Whiting a young seamstress who worked at Rushtons in the early 1900s. Henrietta describes carriages carrying ladies and their maidservants drawing up to either order or collect clothes and other goods.

1890s Rushtons Outfitters.

1890s Cooperative Grocery/Butchers.

1895 Cooperative and Prospect Mill.

1900 Chapel Lane.

1901 Chapel Lane, Main Street corner.

1906 Chapel Lane.

1910 Main Street, Chapel Lane junction.

1950s Chapel Lane from Main Street.

1960s Chapel Lane from Main Street.

1960s Chapel Lane from Quaker Hill.

Clearance

Between 1934 and 1937 there were a number of clearance schemes in central Bingley. Many decaying buildings in Chapel Lane were demolished and the road was widened at the Main Street end.

2016

The current Cooperative presence in Bingley is much smaller than in its heyday when it had major Central Stores buildings on Main Street and shops on Chapel Street. It also had many local shops throughout Bingley and in the majority of local villages and towns. Today it has one supermarket in 5 Rise Shopping Centre.

Chapel Lane also survives, providing a range of smaller shop units and services.

TOP OF TOWN

Atkinson's Joinery

Top of Town was the area on Main Street and the main road leading back towards Cottingley and Nab Wood and which contained shops and pubs. On the right hand side on the road out of Bingley was Atkinson's Milton Mills Joinery Works built there in 1887 and demolished in 2003 to make way for the building of Millwood apartments which first went on sale in 2008.

Kings Head Pub and Myrtle Place

On the same side of the road going back into Bingley was one of Bingley's original coaching inns, the Kings Head (opposite where the Myrtle Grove pub now stands) which was demolished in the late 1960s to make way for the new Bradford and Bingley Headquarters building. Much of Myrtle Place was also demolished during this period for the same reason.

1890 Top of Town, towards Bradford.

Bradford and Bingley Headquarters

Originally on this site stood a low rise three-storey building opened by the then Bingley Building Society in 1962. The merged Bradford and Bingley Building Society (1964) then built their new headquarters on the site between 1972 and 1974. It was abandoned by the building society in 2009 and bought as a development site by Sainsbury's which eventually demolished the building in 2015.

1895 Top of Town, Myrtle Place, Chapel Lane and Mechanics Institute.

1900 Top of Town, King's Head, Myrtle Place, Chapel Lane and Mechanics Institute.

1900 Top of Town from Chapel Lane and Myrtle Place.

1953 Myrtle Cinema looking down from Top of Town.

1960s Looking down from Top of Town at Bingley Building Society building.

1967 to 1971 Kings Head Top of Town.

1980 Aerial of Building Society.

1990s Top of Town looking towards Myrtle Walk shopping centre.

MYRTLE PLACE

Myrtle Place was situated opposite the Main Street end of Chapel Lane until the late 1960s, early 1970s when it was demolished to make way for the new Bradford and Bingley headquarters.

In its time it served Bingley as an open space for events and a market as well as housing the Poorhouse/Workhouse and Police/ Court buildings. Shops and houses were also located in the area.

Myrtle Place Workhouse

In 1726 an old house situated on farmland in what was already named Myrtle Place was converted by the local Vestry Committee into the Bingley Workhouse. In 1776 the Vestry set up a Standing Committee to act as Guardians of the Poor and by 1777 a Parliamentary Report listed local Workhouses (including Bingley) which it suggested had a capacity for up to 40 inmates.

1848 Myrtle Place.

1890 Myrtle Place and the Workhouse.

Myrtle Place Court of Requests and Bingley Courthouse

National legislation again had an effect on Bingley when the Court Baron previously held in the Kings Head Inn for the recovery of small debts was extended by Act of Parliament in 1777. This established a Court of Requests for the recovery of debts under 40 shillings.

Dodd (1958:92) states: *"The growth of business in Bingley – as indicated by the number of small debts to be collected – is indicated by the flourishing state of the Court of Requests. In half a century it had amassed enough in fees to build a Courthouse of its own (1831). This was in Myrtle Place as part of the Kings Head Yard".*

Bingley Lock Up - Myrtle Place

In 1821 a new lock up had been built which adjoined the Workhouse. Part of the funding had been made by the County authorities and part by a loan from the Busfeild Charity locally.

Move of the Court to Keighley

The life of the Court of Requests in Myrtle Place was a short one and in 1839 it was moved to Keighley where in 1847 it became the County Court.

Chartist Drilling in Myrtle Place 1848

On 28th May, 1848, in support of the Chartist cause, a reported 100 men assembled in Myrtle Place for the purpose of drilling and marching. As a result, two of the leaders who had acted as drill sergeants were arrested and later rescued by a mob from the Justice Room at the Brown Cow where they had been appearing before Magistrate William Busfeild Ferrand. This incident became known locally as the Little Siege of Bingley (see Cattell (2011:60) *Bingley and Surrounds - Forgotten Moments from History* for further information).

Move of the Workhouse to Keighley

By 1857 the old Bingley Workhouse had become so dilapidated that the building was condemned and in 1860 the new Union Workhouse in Keighley was ready for the paupers from Bingley to be transferred there.

The 1860 photograph of the Bingley Workhouse and Relieving Office shows the workhouse just prior to demolition. Displayed in the windows are posters showing the Poor Rates.

Building of a New Courthouse in Myrtle Place

Initially, it was proposed that the site of the Workhouse and the lock up (which was out of use) should be acquired by the County authorities. After judicious accounting it was agreed that Bingley Township would have a share of a new building. As a result a brand new Court Building and Police Station was built in 1860 at the expense of the County near the by now disused Court of Requests building.

The new facility served the local community for 60 years until the new Court House and Police Station were built on Bradford Road and occupied in 1929.

Myrtle Place 1860 to 1910

Myrtle Place, apart from its buildings, provided open space for a number of events, some political and some social. Market stalls were allowed until 1892 and then again from 1914 when a market was re-established every Friday.

1860 Bingley Workhouse, Relieving Office and Amalgamated Woolcombers Offices.

1914 Court of Requests/Police Court to left. Lodge to Myrtle Grove Mansion in centre.

1960 Myrtle Place and Old Courthouse on left and Telegraph and Argus offices.

1914 Myrtle Place with Courthouse on left and Lodge to Myrtle Grove in centre.

1960 Myrtle Place.

1967 to 1971 Myrtle Place and Old Building Society office.

A number of formative Independent Labour Party meetings were held in the Place as was a meeting of the Women's Freedom League in 1907. Doubtless other political movements and causes also met in the open space. New entertainment technology also featured when a Cinematographic Exhibition was held in Myrtle Place in the early 1900s.

During this period a number of shops and businesses opened in the Place. Census returns show the establishment of Dunn's Chemists in 1861 and Perfect's Chemists in 1881. By 1901 Harrison's Printers/Stationers and Stoney's Housepainters, Staveley's Tea Shop and Beaton's Butchers had been established. Also recorded is the resident Police Inspector at the Police Station.

The majority of the buildings in Myrtle Place were still, however, residential accomodation for a range of trades and workpeople living and working in Bingley.

Myrtle Place 1920s - The Princess Hall and Swimming Baths

The last civic building constructed in Myrtle Place and the only one still remaining standing in 2016 was the Princess Hall and Swimming Baths opened in 1927. Details of the opening are shown on page 112.

Bradford and Bingley Headquarters

The last remnant of Myrtle Place (apart from the Swimming Pool was pulled down in 1972.

During the year prior to this, building of the new extension to the Bradford and Bingley Building Society Headquarters had commenced and the building was opened in 1974 As such the buildings on Myrtle Place, which had once housed the legal centre of the town, were demolished as part of this redevelopment.

1974 - 2016

In 1974 the new Arts Centre, which is now the home of Bingley Little Theatre, was constructed. In 2012 Bingley Arts Centre was leased by Bingley Little Theatre from Bradford MDC and is now a valued community enterprise.

In 1977 the Jubilee Gardens, in close proximity to the Arts Centre, were built and in 2008 a revamped Town Square was constructed. This now hosts the much diminished Market.

In 1984 Bingley Civic Trust raised funds to return the Butter Cross, Market Hall and Stocks from Prince of Wales Park to the area at the side of the Arts Centre. They also returned the renovated artifacts to Bradford MDC.

1967 to 1971 Telegraph and Argus offices with Princess Hall/ Swimming Pool.

1967 to 1971 Myrtle Place.

2013 Myrtle Place and Bingley Swimming Pool.

PLACES
MYRTLE PARK

Myrtle Grove in the 1970s.

This chapter explores how this well-used facility first came into existence and identifies the events that shaped its development.

Introduction

Any history of Myrtle Park needs to take account of the origins of the site initially as an old farmstead called Spring Head which was bought in 1767 by John Atkinson Busfeild. By 1770 he had erected a substantial mansion called Myrtle Grove. Early visitors to the house included John Wesley who visited and slept there in 1779, calling it a "little paradise".

Owners of Myrtle Grove

By 1837 Bingley was more of an industrial town rather than an agricultural market centre as it had once been. The house changed hands a number of times with the period from 1840 onwards reflecting changes in the social standing of tenants and owners.

1770 John Atkinson Busfeild

1805 Mr Birch bought the house from Busfeild for £10,500

1810 General Twiss

1827 Walker Ferrand (Walter Milligan, 1840s, and Alfred Sharp 1850s and 1860s were tenants)

1874 Alfred Sharp bought Myrtle Grove from Walker Ferrand in 1874 for £13,500 and lived there until 1896

1896 On 2nd November Bingley Co-operative Society bought part of Myrtle Grove (31 acres) to build what was known as Myrtle Pasture garden suburb (or Klondyke as it was nicknamed locally)

1908 Bingley Urban District Council purchased 27 acres to be used as a Public Park

Myrtle Grove.

Transition from a Gentleman's Estate to a Public Park

During this period there was a fairly lengthy but gentle transition from a gentleman's estate which on occasion held public events in adjacent parkland, to a Public Park owned by the town. The parkland was used for public events, many of which still retained a local interest in horticulture and agriculture. Notable events on this theme included:

1837 Institution of two annual fairs held on January 25th for horned cattle and August 25th, 26th, and 27th for horses and merchandise

1852 Gooseberry Show instituted and held for the next 17 years

1861 Floral and Horticultural Show first held at Myrtle Park

1867 First Airedale Agricultural Show held at Myrtle Grove

1869 On August 18th a Gala was held in the grounds of Myrtle Grove with a Band, Dancing and Sports - Bradford Observer report, 1869

1900 Annual Chrysanthemum Show

Myrtle Pasture

Through the efforts of the Bingley Cooperative Society (founded in 1850) Bingley residents were by the 1890s being encouraged to invest in property for the first time. Land for developing local housing stock was expensive but intervention and purchase of land bordering Myrtle Grove by the Cooperative Society enabled them to reduce local land prices. Subsequently the idea of building a garden suburb on Myrtle Pasture became a reality when work on clearing the land commenced in 1895. The first phase of houses were available for occupation at Myrtle Pasture in 1898. West Yorkshire Metropolitan County Council opened Myrtle Park School in 1907 and more phases of houses were built in 1908 and 1913.

The Development of Myrtle Park

Purchase of land for a public park by Bingley Urban District Council in 1908 enabled a substantial tract of land near the town centre to be utilised as a venue for sports, shows, recreation and leisure.

The following timeline demonstrates that many of the facilities and events held nowadays in Myrtle Park owe their origins to similar "happenings" in times past. The timeline is intended to be illustrative, not exhaustive. Detail for the 1920s and 1930s is taken from the Bingley Guardian Yearbook 1936.

1908 On December 23rd, Myrtle Grove and Myrtle Place properties were bought for £7,000 by Bingley Urban District Council. The area of 27.5 acres was purchased for use as a Public Park

1912 Sheepdog trials were run every July in Myrtle Park. Band Concerts and "sings" in Park were also held

1912 Childrens Corner.

1912 Rose Garden.

1914 Old Children's Corner.

1914.

1918.

1918.

1913 Cast Iron Covered bandstand erected in Myrtle Park manufactured by Walter Macfarlane and Co, Saracen Foundry, Glasgow. Cost £270.

1916 Open air performance of the 'Masque of Wool' play in celebration of Bingley's agricultural and industrial history

1921 Bingley War Memorial unveiled September 17th by J.H. Robinson, of Greenhill Hall. The Memorial was designed by Mr A.Bolton and built by J.H.Clarke and Sons, Bingley

1921 Bowling Green and three Hard Tennis Courts provided at a cost of £725

1923 Offices of Town Clerk and Surveyor transferred from Bingley Mechanics Institute and Town Hall to Myrtle Grove in July

1923 Armistice Day Parade first held

1923 Small Pavilion and Convenience provided for a cost of £620

1924 Second Bowling Green provided for a cost of £620

1924 Footpath and Footbridge over the river. Cost £1,217

1924 - 1928 Motor Cycle Gymkhanas held

1926 Myrtle Grove became the Town Hall and the remainder of offices were transferred there

1928 Miniature golf course provided

1928 Refreshment pavilion built. Cost £1,000

1929 Games apparatus purchased. Cost £100

1931 Brass band concerts begun in 1913 were discontinued

1932 Annual Music Festival begins

1933 Myrtle Park Bowls Club founded

1936 A children's paddling pool was built

1942 Music Festival resumed in 1942 as a Children's Concert

1945 7270 acres of land in Brown Cow Field were presented to Bingley UDC by Hempel Brothers (Bingley) as an extension to Myrtle Park

1947 "White Rose Rally" for Bingley, Keighley and Shipley Local Associations of Boy Scouts held and attended by the Chief Scout, Lord Rowallan, at Myrtle Park, with a camp on the St. Ives estate. There was also a Scouts Own service in Myrtle Park with music provided by the Haworth Public Prize Band, a Scout Rally and march past

1948 Annual Children's Gala held at Myrtle Park

1950 From the 1950s there were: two bowling greens, three hard tennis courts and a children's playground

1951 Bridge built across the Aire at Myrtle Park to commemorate the Festival of Britain. The bridge was manufactured by Takewrights Ltd (Liverpool/Newport)

1966 Toddlers playground provided. Cost £60

1970 First Bingley Bonfire in November organised by Bingley Round Table and run by them until 2002

1991 First Music at Myrtle

1998 to 2005 Pulse Party in the Park

2005 Petition to Bradford MDC for improved Children's Play facilities

2002 to 2011 Bingley Bonfire organised by Baildon and District Round Table and was organised by Bingley Airedale Rotary Club from 2011

2006 to 2016 Bingley Music Live held in September

2008 New Children's Adventure Playground. £25,000 Grant fromWREN

2009 Bingley Skate Park opened May (Myrtle Park Street Plaza)

2009 Bingley Gala revived after a period of 10 years

2012 Bingley Agricultural Show cancelled due to bad weather for the first time in 146 years

Reflecting on the success of Myrtle Park

What the timeline reveals is the major investment made in the park during the 1920s and 1930s as a local resource. What it also highlights are the efforts made over the last 20 years to provide local community events which profile Bingley and attract people from further afield.

The addition of the new skate park and children's playground built on the legacy established 108 years ago to provide green space close to the town centre as a heritage for Bingley residents. What are your memories?

BINGLEY FIRE STATION

Historically, fire fighting was dealt with at a local level only, with fire fighters unable to travel outside their parish or village boundaries to respond to a fire or an emergency. It was even a common occurrence for fire pumps to be sponsored by an insurance company. This brought its own unique challenges because if you were not insured by the company that owned the pump sent to deal with the fire, it could be turned around and the property left to burn.

First Bingley Brigade

The first Bingley Brigade was formed by the Bingley Improvement Commissioners who had been appointed to improve services within the town in 1847. They bought their first fire engine in 1850 at a cost of £31. From that date until 1902 stables for the horse-drawn engine were provided by the Commissioners on their land at Leonard Street but fire engines were kept at Myrtle Place.

As you might expect, from the time the hand fire bell in Main Street was rung and the horses were united with the engine in Myrtle Place, critical time for the control of any fire had passed.

In 1850, the first Bingley Fire Brigade was engaged. The Superintendant was paid two guineas a year and the six firemen were paid a shilling for attendance at a monthly parade and a shilling for attendance

at fires. The service was intended to pay for itself and a charge of half a guinea was made for the use of the fire engine locally, or a guinea outside the district.

Another new fire engine was bought in 1861 for £120, however no mention of uniforms being supplied is made until 1863 about the supply of "suitable regimentals, including helmets".

The Bradford Observer reported a major fire at Providence Mill, Bingley in December, 1861, which was attended by *"Bingley Fire Brigade with their new and powerful engine and also their old engine"*.

New Fire Brigade

Things appear to have developed well until 1870 when the Old Fire Brigade was disbanded and a New Fire Brigade was formed. No reason was suggested for this in the history records that I initially investigated.

However my research into Improvement Commissioner meeting notes identified that this was because firemen refused to work with their Superintendant and vice versa. Notes of the next meeting state that firemen's retainers/wages had been improved. No doubt this early example of withdrawing labour to gain increased money was the real reason for the dispute!

In 1872 the brigade bought its first large steam powered fire engine made by Shand Mason and which cost £722. Bingley was among the first towns in the West Riding to equip its brigade with a steam fire engine.

Major Fire Drill

The Brigade held a major fire drill in 1874 the Bradford Observer, September 5th, reported the event and its success: *"On Thursday last, a year having passed without a fire taking place in the district to test the efficiency of the Fire Brigade, the fire bell was rung by Superintendent Isaac Wood. The object was to see how soon water could be laid upon premises situated a quarter of a mile distant from the fire engine house in Myrtle Place.*

No sooner had the bell been rung than a number of men were on the spot and the hand-pushed hose reel cart was despatched. Water was delivered from the mains six-and-a-half minutes from the first sound of the bell.

The steam fire engine arrived on the scene of action 13 and-a-half minutes later and was distributing volumes of water through 230 yards of hose in 18 and-a-half minutes. The Superintendent and all but two of his men (who did not hear the fire bell), were present. This is all the more satisfactory as not the slightest intention had been given to the firemen that their services would be required".

Change

A Union of Fire Brigades nationally was inaugurated in 1887.

In 1894 Bingley governance changed from control by the Improvement Commissioners to Bingley Urban District Council.

In June 1899 a public demonstration of fire equipment was held in Bingley, organised by the Fire Brigades Union. The Leeds Mercury,

June 26th, 1899 reported: *"Crowds of folks poured into Bingley to witness the passage through the streets of fire engines and firemen and the frequent ringing of the fire bell close at hand. Bingley had been singled out for a display in the form of Yorkshire Brigades belonging to the National Fire Brigades Union and an exhibition of drills.*

The display took place by kind permission of Mr W Ferrand, of St Ives in the prettily situated field adjoining the Brown Cow Inn. The participants were from Bingley, Rotherham, Bradford, Goole, Conisborough and Low Fold, Leeds.

Mr Herbert Sharp, of Bingley, commented that some public authorities did not realise the importance of fully equipping their brigades so that they could deal efficiently with large fires. In his own town, Bingley, he was pleased to say that the Fire Brigade had for some years been in a good position but it was an admitted fact that the premises they occupied were not altogether suitable to enable their work to be done as it ought to be done".

Exhibitions were then given by all the brigades with equipment lent by Bingley, namely a dry steamer engine, manual engine, hose cart and hydrant.

At the end of the programme the various teams numbering about 70 persons adjourned to the Brown Cow where they sat down to a substantial tea".

Herbert Sharp, a local politician and relative of one of Bingley's most renowned benefactors, obviously had some local influence and a point to make about the lack of an adequate fire station.

New Fire Station

By 1902 a new fire station had been built on Market Street (now the site of the Suburban Bar) by Bingley Urban District Council. Facilities included stables for the horses pulling the fire engines and a house for the superintendent.

Further equipment was bought in:

1913 A large Dennis motor fire engine ....Cost £1,000
and escape ladder

1928 A small Dennis motor fire engine .... Cost £821

1935 A large Dennis motor fire engine .... Cost £1,290

The old steam fire engine bought in 1872 was still in use in 1935.

National Fire Service - 1941

In the late 1930s and with the threat of war across Europe, the Home Office began to re-organise Britain's fire services, and thousands of volunteers joined the Auxiliary Fire Service and Women's Voluntary Service for Air Raid Precautions (later Women's Royal Voluntary Service).

A new National Fire Service, was formed in 1941 and membership of the Fire Brigades Union rose from 3,000 in 1939 to almost 70,000 in 1942.

The Fire Station tower at Bingley, which had always housed a fire warning bell, was also fitted with an air raid siren during the war.

Move of the Fire Station

In 1973 the Fire Station was moved to its present site in the Old Railway Yard on Keighley Road, Bingley, where in 1974 it became part of the West Yorkshire Fire and Rescue Service.

1964.

Listing of the Old Fire Station

In 1985 the Old Fire Station was granted Grade II Listing by English Heritage (now Historic England). This described the building as two storeys high with a four-storey tower on which there is an open wooden structure originally for hanging hoses for drying.

During 2002 an Architectural Building Recording was carried out by Haigh (2002) for English Heritage which stated that as of 2002: *"Archaeological building recording of the Old Fire Station was carried out by Stephen Haigh, prior to its redevelopment as a bar/restaurant. The building dates from around 1902 and contained space for three fire engines and a workshop, former stables, a recreation room, hose-drying tower, as well as the original superintendent's house. The building recording involved both drawn and photographic survey, copies of which are on file in West Yorkshire Historic England Register".*

1970s.

THE HISTORY OF MILNER FIELD FARM

While much has been written on the history of Milner Field Estate, nothing has been written or researched on the history of Milner Field Farm. This chapter represents my research into the farm during 2016. It is intended to lodge this new research with Shipley College, Saltaire Archives for academic and historical purposes.

Family hay-making with Milner Field Mansion in background.

Milner Field Estate

Work on building Milner Field mansion for Titus Salt Junior commenced in 1871 and took two years to complete, the building having been designed by Thomas Harris, of London.

Indentures

There are two Indentures in the Bradford Archives which besides identifying transfer of land ownership also establish agricultural farming being carried out on the land prior to Titus Salt Junior building Milner Field Mansion.

1868 Indenture

Between Arthur Duncombe and Titus Salt and witnessed by Charles Evans of 6, Grays Chambers, High Holborn, London. (same address as Thomas Harris the Architect, of Milner Field Mansion).

1. Barn, Mistal, Stable, Garden
2. Farmhouse, Garden, Cottage

4 Rough Ings each with 10 days work

8th July 1869 Indenture

Between Titus Salt of Crow Nest and Titus Salt the Younger.

"All the several messuages or dwelling houses, farm buildings, closes of land and plantations in the township of Gilstead, parish of Bingley, County of Yorkshire – Milner Field Estate containing 58 acres, one rood and 35 perches and plantations containing 20 acres, three roods and eleven perches".

Reference to grazing of ewes is also made in the indenture.

Builders

While the mansion house was built by local builders and masons Shaftoe and Barry, of York, the gardens, woods and landscaped park incorporating Milner Field Farm, were designed by Robert Marnock, the renowned Victorian gardener and landscape designer, famous for his "gardenesque" style of design.

Robert Marnock

The Gardener's Magazine (November 23rd, 1889) describes Marnock as *"the most talented landscape gardener of modern time"*. Mc Kinna in Van den Daele and Beale (2011:174) identifies that Marnock laid out the grounds and park at Milner Field in 1870 and probably also the kitchen garden.

Milner Field Farm

The Building News Magazine of December 22nd, 1876, describes the mansion and gardens and also makes reference to the estate including the farm - *"at the lower end of the park are model farm buildings"*. Wooler (2015:18) states: *"This source indicates that by 1876 Milner Field Farm appears to have been constructed, given a time period between 1865 and 1876 for its construction"*.

Agricultural Show Awards

A report in the Leeds Mercury of April 20th, **1872**, refers to the Manager at Titus Salt Junior's farm and Milner Field estate winning a *prize for short-horned cattle*. This is the earliest reference of the existence of the farm on the new estate. An advertisement in the same newspaper on June 18th, 1872, *states "To Butchers. For SALE at Milner Field 30 prime fat shorthorn BULLOCKS in lots to suit purchasers. Can be seen by applying to the Bailiff at the farm"* On 30th November, **1874** the Bradford Observer recorded that Milner Field Farm had won awards for showing six Fat Cattle at the Birmingham Cattle Show.

This places the building of the farm at a date before 1876.

Aerial showing U-shaped Model Farm at Milner Field.

A Model Farm

Wooler (2015:19) also suggests that Milner Field Farm appears to represent a model farmstead because of *"the symmetry of the structures, suggestive of farm buildings that were erected at the same time"*. Wooler (2015:27) further identifies Milner Field Farm as a model farm which was built and planned as a complete unit.

Historical context is established by Healey (1885:124) in *A Series of Picturesque Views and Country Houses,* when making the reference *"at the lower end of the park are model farm buildings"*. This is essentially a reiteration of the comment made in The Building News Magazine in 1876 and is specific about it being a model farm.

Van den Daele and Beale (2011:130) reference a sale catalogue for Milner Field Estate which describes the buildings on the farm as *"a substantially built Farm House (with Dairy) and Farm buildings with Sheds, Stables, Mistals (Milking Sheds), Cow Byres, Fattening Byres, Barns, Granary, Cart Sheds, Open Sheds, Poultry Houses etc"*. Besides the Farmhouse, Lodge and Grounds the 78.546 acres of farmland included arable land, woodland and grass and part of the Coach Road leading to Milner Field Mansion.

Model Farm Definition

Wade-Martins (2002:1) suggests that *"A model farm can be defined as a steading built for a landowner who wanted to set an example to the tenantry on his estate and society at large"*.

This definition is expanded on below in terms of an Historic England research project into model farmsteads: *"Planned and model farmsteads were of a peculiarly British type. They were frequently illustrated in books and journals of the period, and their designs were sometimes exported to other countries which were inspired by our agricultural revolution of the late 18th and 19th centuries"*.

They were built by and for landed estates, which played a prominent role in agricultural improvement. The term 'model farm' was not used until the mid 19th century, and it was commonly coined for the farmstead of the 'home farm' closest to the great house of an estate.

Planned Layouts

Many farmsteads in this period were planned to courtyard layouts, but estates commissioned land agents, architects and engineers to design some spectacular 'set-piece' designs which advertised not only the wealth and status of their owners, often derived from industry and commerce, but also their interest in the latest innovations in applied science, agriculture and engineering.

As such farm buildings were arranged on industrial 'flow-line' principles the model farm being designed to: *"Increase efficiency and minimise labour while improving conditions for livestock in order to increase efficiency and output"* (Clarke 2011:51).

Model Farms were built to specific planned layouts as shown below:

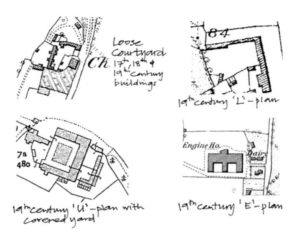

In her survey of Milner Field Farm, Wooler (2015:27) observes: *"To the east of the house there is a U-shaped plan of farm buildings of single storey".* This would appear to identify the model as a 19th Century "U" plan.

Innovations

Milner Field Farm was built as the "home farm" to Titus Salt Junior's substantial estate which in turn was built from the wealth derived from industry and commerce and success of the business in Saltaire. Innovations on the estate included telephone, electricity, heating and ventilation, drainage systems, water cooled dairies/larders and automatic fodder hoists.

On October 12th, 1872, the Leeds Mercury and York Herald announced that the Yorkshire Agricultural Society had elected Titus Salt Junior, of Milner Field, a Life Member in recognition of his interest and approach to farming on the estate.

Salts Model Village

Given that Titus Salt's vision was of a **model village** (now recognised as a World Heritage site), then his son's approach to complementing this approach at his adjoining estate by commissioning a **model farm** to be built was unsurprising. It shows a congruence of purpose in which the two should not be considered as separate entities, but as part of the same vision.

Using Milner Field to Profile Saltaire

Titus Salt Junior organised two major visits by members of the Royal Family both of which involved them staying at Milner Field and enjoying Titus's lavish hospitality. The first was by Their Royal Highnesses The Prince and Princess of Wales - the future King Edward V11 and Queen Alexandra between the 22nd and 24th of June, 1882. The second was by Princess Beatrice, of Battenberg, and her husband, Henry, on 6th May 1887, when they opened the Royal Yorkshire Jubilee Exhibition which Titus had organised in Saltaire to showcase British industry and commerce.

Feeding the Royals was a key aspect of each visit. Milner Field was designed to cater for both exotic and more simple tastes. The main house had a conservatory attached to it as an orangery and seating area. The kitchen garden and greenhouses had a vinery, melon house, fig house, pineapple house, ice house, many varieties of fruit trees and also a mushroom cellar. This was a source for the more exotic culinary offerings.

Within the grounds there was also a fishing lake which a later resident of the mansion, Sir James Roberts, would stock with trout. Milner

Field Farm was able to provide more basic and staple fare in terms of dairy produce, eggs, grain, poultry and beef.

As such Milner Field provided a perfect local and integrated backdrop for visitors to enjoy while visiting Saltaire.

Tenancy of Milner Field Farm and Milner Field Farm Lodge
The Salt Years

An advertisement in The Leeds Mercury of Saturday, January 24th, 1880, gives some clues as to the stock kept on the farm and a change to the farm having a tenant instead of employing a manager.

T. Dodds and Son - Auctioneers and Tenant - right Valuers - Wakefield

Home Farm, Milner Field, one mile from Saltaire Station

Sale of seven Milch Cows (in calf and lately calved), two Curt Brood Mares (both stinted from "Young Tom") Cart Horse, Six Shropshire Ewes (in lamb to pure-bred Shropshire ram), four Shropshire Ewe Lambs, two Shropshire rams, ninety half-bred ewes and shearlings (in lamb to Shropshire ram, nine store pigs, one Sow, about fifteen tons of hay and a few tons of turnips and mangels, a large quantity of Farming Implements which may have only been used for a short time, and by the best makers. Portable Steam Engine, Grinding Mill.

T. Dodds and Son are instructed by Titus Salt Esq (who has let the Home Farm) to sell by Auction on Friday, February 6th, 1880, the above stock.

Home Farm, Milner Field, one mile from Saltaire Station.
Sale of seven Milch Cows (in calf and lately calved), two Cart Brood Mares (both stinted to "Young Tom"), Cart Horse, six Shropshire Ewes (in lamb to pure-bred Shropshire ram), four Shropshire Ewe Lambs, two Shropshire Rams, 90 half-bred Ewes and Shearlings (in lamb to Shropshire ram), nine Store Pigs, one Sow, about 15 tons of Hay, and a few tons of Turnips and Mangels, a large quantity of Farming Implements, which have only been used a short time, and are by the best makers; Portable Steam Engine, Grinding Mill, &c.
T. DODDS and SON are instructed by Titus Salt, Esq. [who has let the Home Farm], to Sell by Auction, on *Friday, February Sixth,* 1880, the above-named STOCK.
Sale to commence at eleven o'clock.
Catalogues on application.

The week before the above newspaper advertisement, the same newspaper on January, 19th, 1880, carried another specific to the machinery mentioned in the advertisement a week later: *"To be sold a*

5 Horse Power Portable engine by Marshall and Sons, Gainsborough. Been little used and condition equal to new. Either separately or with grinding mill, chaff cutter, cake mill etc. Apply John McKie. The Farm, Milner Field, Bingley". This equipment was used to prepare straw, hay and foodstuff to feed to farm livestock.

John McKie is identified in the 1871 Census as a farm bailiff working near Crewe, Cheshire. In the 1881 Census he and his family are living in East Yorkshire and his occupation is described as farm bailiff - unemployed. In later documentation for the marriage of one of his daughters his occupation is described as Estate Factor. His wife, Catherine, and he had three children born in Bingley in 1876, 1878 and 1881. It is therefore safe to assume that he was the farm manager mentioned in the newspaper article of April, 1872, and the Bailiff mentioned in the advertisement of June, 1872, and that his unemployed status in 1881 was due to change from management to tenancy of the farm.

Links between Milner Field and Milner Field Farm

An entry written by Catherine Salt (Titus Junior's wife) in her day diary for February, 1880, lists farm dairy equipment and is presumably intended for inventory purposes associated with the let of the same date, shown above. Included are: *1 Butter tub for making up, 4 large spirited milk cans with lids ,4 smaller ditto, 1 Strainer, 1 ditto for putting cream into, 2 piggins (milking pails), 2 measures, 1 churn, 1 wood frame, 4 tin bowls, 9 pot bowls, 1 weighing machine, 1 pair steps, 2 baskets.*

Tenants

Census, Electoral Roll and Tax Records show that there has been considerable continuity as regards tenancy of the farm and farm lodge. George Cattle is shown as having been the tenant of the farm from 1881 to 1894 with two farm labourers and a domestic servant. Newspaper reports show that George Cattle won awards for his sheep at the Wharfedale Agricultural Show in (York Herald, May 12th, 1883) and for Breed Cattle at the Airedale Agricultural Show (York Herald August 31st, 1883).

Frederick Allen followed him and is shown in the 1901 Census as a farmer living at the farm with his wife and four children. Thomas Booth a farm labourer, and his family are shown in the 1881, 1891 and 1901 Census returns as living at Milner Field Farm Lodge.

The Roberts Years
The Downs Family - Custodians and Continuity

The Yorkshire Post and Leeds Intelligencer of August 10th, 1901, announced that the farm was to be let, presumably at the end of

Frederick Allen's tenancy. *"To Let with entry to land February 1902, house and buildings May 1, 1902 - Milner Field Farm Bingley containing 16 acres grass and 16 arable: excellent house and buildings suitable for dairy farming. For further details apply H C Salt, Milner Field, Bingley* (Harold Crossley Salt).

Downs' family recollections appear to show that John Downs applied for and was successful in gaining tenancy of the farm in 1902.

In 1903, Sir James Roberts bought Milner Field and the Estate. This concurred with John Downs, shown in the 1901 Census as a farmer on the Nook Farm in Wilsden being part of the Milner Field Farm tenancy. Select Tax Records (1907 to 1922) on the land show that he was assessed as having to pay 18 shillings and fourpence a year rent to James Roberts on an annual land assessment value of £220.

His sons, Hartley and James Ernest, are also shown in the West Yorkshire Electoral Registers during the periods 1909 to 1940 and 1919 to 1930 as living at either Milner Field Farm or Milner Field Farm Lodge.

Keith and Pam Downs and their son, David, and his wife, Stella, continue farming the land 114 years after John Downs first moved to Milner Field Farm.

Conclusion

The farm is part of a historic context, landscape and agricultural setting dating back over 140 plus years. Its location tangibly links industry and agriculture together during what Barnwell and Giles (1997) describe as the "boom" years for British agriculture in respect of what was termed "high farming" between 1850 and 1870. "High farming" was described as the application of science and technology to farming.

The proximity of the model farm to the model village and the fact that it is still fulfilling the agricultural purpose for which it was originally designed are worthy of historical consideration.

The landscape links to notable landscape designer Robert Marnock and the further links to Royal patronage of the Milner Field Estate and the part that Milner Field Farm undoubtedly played are unique aspects of not only local, but national history.

Postscript
Links to Farming

While both the Salts and Roberts are best known locally for their manufacturing enterprises at Saltaire, my further research has revealed links in both families to farming and model farms.

The Salts

Four of Titus Salt Senior's sons were involved in farming in some form. Records for 1861 show that Titus Salt Senior and Herbert were Life Members of the Royal Agricultural Society of England. In 1861 **Herbert** and **Titus (Junior)** were the only two sons still living at home and had plenty of opportunity to exchange experience and ideas together.

Census records for 1861 show Herbert as a Farmer of 360 acres employing six men at Methley Park where he farmed up until 1867. The 1871 Census shows Herbert as a farmer of 450 acres employing 10 men and four boys at Thorns Farm on the Beaulieu Estate in Hampshire, where he farmed until 1873. He was recognised as both a respected judge at Agricultural Shows and an exhibitor, particularly of shorthorn cattle.

It is entirely possible that Herbert picked up pointers for setting up a model farm from his Beaulieu experience (which had such a home farm), and passed these on to his brothers **Edward** and Titus Junior who subsequently set up model farms at Ferniehurst, Baildon, and Milner Field.

Herbert continued to farm and exhibit cattle locally from 1876 until 1885 having moved to Carla Beck, Skipton.

Eldest brother **William Henry Salt** is shown in 1881 Census as a farmer employing 10 men on 400 acres at Mapplewell Grange, Leicestershire.

Harold Crossley Salt, the second son of Titus Salt Junior and the person shown on the sale advertisement of 1901 as representing Catherine Salt in the sale of Milner Field Farm, attended the Royal Agricultural College in 1894 and 1895 and at the time of his marriage in 1906 was working as Land Agent at Barrington Manor, Burford, in the Cotswolds.

While having more than a passing interest in farming it is likely that William Henry, Edward and Titus Jr had interests in many other areas, while Herbert devoted much of his time to farming and Harold to Land Agency.

The Roberts

James Roberts, later to be Sir James Roberts and manufacturer at Saltaire was born in Haworth. The 1871 Census show his father, James, as a tenant farmer of 12 acres near Haworth and in 1881 as a retired farmer near Haworth.

Right to Left, Nick Salt, David and Stella Downs and Alan at Milner Field Farm, May 2016.

Model Farm in Jersey

One of Sir James's sons, Joseph Henry Nicholson Roberts otherwise known in the family as Harry (age 30), was seriously wounded in France in 1917 during World War I. Although he survived he was thought to be too infirm to carry on the Saltaire business. He went on to marry and lived a comfortable life as a farmer in Jersey until his death in 1946. In 1924 he set up a model farm.

Local press reported: *"He laid the foundations of a unique model farm that has earned the reputation of being one of the best equipped estates in the British Isles.*

There are now over 100 head of prize cattle at Vinchelez (his home). Every known electrical and mechanical device is used in the housing and feeding of the animals while close by stands the perfectly equipped dairy where a special staff prepare milk, cream, butter and cheese which is so well known to residents of this island".

Knowledge

In 2016 Milner Field Farm, run by the Downs family as tenant farmers, is the last dairy farm in the Bingley area.

While there are elements of conjecture on my part, there are tangible links within and between the Salt, Roberts and Downs families with regard to knowledge of dairy farming and model farms. I sense that historically this knowledge has been shared, put into practice and passed across from each generation to the next, and that we are only now realising the full extent of this.

Thanks to the Downs family for providing family photographs of work on the farm from their archives.

BINGLEY TEACHER TRAINING COLLEGE FOR WOMEN

Bingley Teacher Training College was opened by West Riding County Council in 1911 as a result of Government intervention to formalise the training of women teachers. Ownership of the land and choice of site for the college are outlined in this chapter as is comment about its early days, opening and eventual closure.

Land in Bingley

Bingley Grammar School was endowed in 1529 and during this early period also acquired land in Bingley area to provide education and the "maintenance of a schoolmaster". This included the purchase of what came to be known as Lady House Farm around 1570.

The farm was owned by Bingley Grammar from this period until 1908 when the school sold the land for £1,500 to the West Riding County

Council for the building of Bingley Teacher Training College. The farm building was described as being an old building with mullioned windows and a stone roof. It is likely that Lady Lane (originally Lady Farm Lane) which was the approach road to the college was named so because of its relationship to the farm.

Commissioning the College

The County Council had spent considerable time inspecting as many as 50 sites in what was a keen struggle for selection. On January 31st, 1908, it was reported in the Bingley Chronicle that after consideration of a short list of 11 sites (at Baildon, Bingley, Brighouse, Calverley, Elland, Gildersome, Hawarth, Otley, Sandal, Shipley, and Stainland), Bingley had been recommended by the West Riding County Council, as the site for the new college.

The architect for the project was Mr J. Vickers Edwards, Architect to the West Riding County Council. He had reported that the Bingley location **was a good one**, somewhat **elevated and uneven**, but approached by **good roads**.

The Site

The site consisted of **meadowland** and **farm buildings** which occupied one end of the estate. Other meadows adjoining could be bought if required. Drainage, water and gas supply were good and although as stated, the land rose to a certain extent, a very suitable plateau could be obtained for the erection of the college.

The site of the college was most commonly described at the time as lying pleasantly on the sunny slope that encloses Bingley to the North and occupying a commanding position overlooking the valley, with a sweep of moorland just above.

In June, 1908, sketch plans for the proposed hostels and main block were considered and passed.

Rivalry

Unfortunately, the rivalry to provide a site also brought with it undercurrents of grumbling about the **cost** and consequent extravagance of the project. At stake was the **commercial potential** for each area to benefit from the **stimulus in local trade** that would be provided by 200 young lady students being added to the local population. The eventual total cost of land, buildings and equipment for the college was £80,648.

Buildings

In March, 1909, contracts for the building operations were agreed and on Friday, March 19th, 1909, an article in the Bingley Chronicle gave details of the shape, size and location of the college buildings and what uses they were going to be put to.

In total, seven buildings were erected, namely the main college building, the five halls of residence, and a bath block (plans originally including a swimming bath) a bakehouse, a gymnasium, boiler rooms and washhouse. The residential halls were named after individuals considered to be prominent educationalists across history, namely Hild, Alcuin, Ascham, Priestley, and Acland.

With the prospect of a substantial new building in the area some uninformed Bingley residents who saw it growing were puzzled and wondered what the buildings were going to be. One day after driving a party past the scene of activity, a coachman was heard to observe: *"We've been round to look at t' new Asylum!"*.

This comment was no doubt inspired by the fact that West Riding County had built a County Asylum at nearby Menston in 1884 (the architect being J. Vickers Edwards, who also drew up the plans for the College.

Foundation Stones

The foundation stones for the college and its five residential halls were laid on May 24th, 1909. The ceremony, held in fine weather, started after tea had been served in a marquee on the borders of the moor close to the Market Hall and Butter Cross, situated in Prince of Wales Park in 1888.

The ceremony was interrupted several times by suffragettes heckling Walter Runciman, President of the Board of Education, during his opening speech. A prominent Liberal Peer he retorted:

"In this college women will not only be taught to teach, but they will be taught good manners".

Resuming his speech he was again heckled by one suffragette with a shout of: *"Votes for women"*.

He responded by stating: *"I hope that the young lady will realise that we are met to found an institution for the education of women".*

The ceremony then moved to the actual college site about a quarter of a mile away. On the way back from the park to the college site the suffragettes again tried to approach Runciman. This time they were kept away by the police as they did not have tickets for the ceremony and were not allowed into the college grounds. At the gate however, one of the more persistent suffragettes called out: *"We have to decide about the education of children as well as the men, tax and representation go together as a Liberal principle. Down with the Liberal Government".*

To the last remark one of the dignitaries quickly retorted: *"And up with the Independent Labour Party",* which met with laughter from all present.

First Principal

The post of Principal was advertised in December, 1910, and initially, there were 42 applicants. After a rigorous process of selection, Dr Helen Wodehouse, a lecturer in Philosophy at Birmingham University, was the successful candidate. In May, 1911, the decision was made to appoint her.

Miss Wodehouse arrived in Bingley a month before the students and took a room at the Midland Hotel (now Maverick's) her reason being:

"In order to keep an eye on my responsibilities on the hill. There seemed a good many in the shape of scaffolding and whitewash pails but my influence over them seemed remarkably small".

First Students

On October 2nd, 1911, the first students (102 in total) came into residence, 22 for one year only as they had already passed the Board of Education Teachers' Certificate Examination. An article in the Keighley News on October 7th reported the arrival of the students as follows: *"Monday was the first day when the students arrived and it was clear to those who kept their eyes open that they were arriving. The signs were a stream of female teachers making their way up Park Road to the College, some of them carrying their bags, while an unusual number of trunks, bags and valises left at the railway station indicated that others had chosen not to encumber themselves with their luggage on the uphill walk. Instead they preferred to leave it to be conveyed to the college by other and, as far as they were concerned, easier methods.*

Now that such a considerable number of young lady students are settled in the institution, the task of the postman who serves the district should be harder than before, for young ladies are known to better correspondents than most people. Perhaps the increase of business which will follow at Bingley Post Office will help to awaken the slow moving authorities a little to the necessity for a new and convenient office for the place. (This eventually happened in 1914).

The people in the town, by the way, have not yet become accustomed to the spectacle of the lights on a part of the hillside where lights were not seen before at night. They have been pointed out again and again during the past few days as 'the college lights', and will be until the novelty wears off".

Reminiscing 54 years later a former student, E.R. Ellis, speaking in 1965, remembers being among the first group of students to start at the College:

"Fifty-four years ago in October 1911 about one hundred of us came to Bingley. On a warm sunny day we had our first sight of the lovely buildings on the hill and we were charmed. There was a spaciousness that was wonderful. We each had a room of our own; the views were inspiring. There were trees and a stream meandering through the grounds. It was a peaceful setting in a peaceful England, three years before the outbreak of the First World War".

Opening of the College

The opening of the college was later than planned due to an extremely bad winter in 1910 which hampered the building programme. The opening eventually took place on October 21st, 1911, a day of rainy and inclement weather.

The principle speaker was Sir John Horsfall, the Chairman of the West Riding County Council. Among the most remembered speeches was that of Helen Wodehouse who ended her speech by concluding that she hoped that: *"Mental fresh air and mental sunshine would be developed in the students through their association with green woods and purple moors and the sight of a valley full of stars at night".*

The latter words and image would be included in the College Song, written in 1914 and repeated by students across the years to describe the beauty of the College location:

Bingley College Song

First Verse

"A valley full of stars at night, day's mist and evenings deep blue light. These surely must inspire; all who dwell on Bingley's hill, Or tramp the purple moors at will. Come show the world your fire."

Further Memories

Further memories for the period 1911 to 1932 will be included in Section Four, page 181 of this book in which former student Doris Reeve (1926 - 1928) recounts her time at the college and the impact it had on her.

The College - Later Years

Due to Government cutbacks in teacher training the Bingley College site closed in 1978 after 67 years in which it is estimated that it trained in excess of 15,000 teachers. Latterly it trained both female and male students with an intake of 900.

The main college building and five halls of residence still stand in their prominent position overlooking Bingley, two of the halls being residential care homes and the others apartments and flats. While the halls still overlook fields at the rear, the grounds to the front have been developed as detached houses.

An ex-Bingley College student, John Harvey, still runs a website which can be accessed at www.bingleycollege.co.uk

In 2009 John and I under the banner of Friends of Bingley College organised a reunion of former students and staff to mark the centenary of the laying of the foundation stones. Some 250 people actually turned up for the weekend celebrations held in Bingley and which included a walk over the moors.

So, it would appear that the college may be gone but is definitely not forgotten!

BINGLEY'S LOST CINEMAS - WHAT HAPPENED TO THEM?

Smithy, prior to demolition in 1913.

Introduction

The first regular cinema recorded in Bingley was in a building behind the market in Main Street and later (circa 1907) came shows in the Victoria Hall and in the Co-operative Assembly Rooms.

Between 1911 and 1922 Picture Palaces as they were originally known opened in Bingley, Baildon, Keighley, Shipley and Saltaire and were to provide entertainment to all age groups over the next 50 years.

This chapter traces the history of the two main cinemas in Bingley from opening to closure to establish what happened to them.

Memories

A couple of weeks ago I took my youngest son and a friend to "the movies" or as I used to know them, the pictures. Our trip involved a car journey, a train journey and a walk to see one "movie", a lot of advertisements and a visit to the bank manager to finance the popcorn!

At one time Bingley, like other towns and cities had two main local cinemas serviced by local sweet shops and fish and chip shops. Each was frequented regularly by a local population eager to catch up with the films of the day, sometimes two or three times a week for a minimal charge for circle or stall seats, no mortgage involved!

The main venues in Bingley were:

The Hippodrome Cinema

This was the first main cinema to be built in Bingley which was opened in 1913 on the demolished site of Longbottom's Blacksmith's situated on the right of Main Street past the Old Queen Heads Hotel. The photograph heading this chapter shows the Smithy prior to demolition with a sign announcing "Site for Picture Palace - Bingley Hippodrome Ltd".

The cinema was opened by Michael P. Cryer with a seating capacity of 739 and was eventually the first in Bingley to introduce "talkie" films. In its heyday it had two shows nightly and two changes of film per week.

The Hippodrome in 1915.

Did the Music Match the Action?

Fred Hoyle (later Sir Fred Hoyle,) a famous academic, astronomer, author and broadcaster from Bingley recounted in his 1986 (page nine) book *The Small World of Fred Hoyle* that his mother was a pianist at the cinema circa 1916. Her job was to accompany the silent films. As a Royal Academy trained musician she preferred to play classical pieces which did not always fit well with the action and storyline of some of the films of the period. Consequently her musical tastes did not match those of the cinema manager and she left. A week later the manager asked her to go back to her job because of a decline in attendances. When cinemagoers were asked why? they told the manager "We didn't come to see your films, we came to hear Mrs Hoyle play!"

The Hippodrome continued to show silent films until February, 1930. During that month the cinema featured two of the first 'talkies' namely Al Jolson's *Sonny Boy* and *There's A Rainbow Round My Shoulder.*

Heyday then Closure

The 1930s and 1940s saw the establishing of the Hollywood era of film making and film stars followed by the development of post war musicals and action films. The early 50s are remembered by many as a period when cowboy films featuring the likes of Alan Ladd and John Wayne

came to the fore, particularly for children. Margaret Flaherty, who worked at the Hippodrome as an usherette in the 1950s remembers that the cinema was still very busy, especially on Saturday nights. With this being the case, she and other staff could not understand why the Hippodrome closed down, showing its last film in 1953.

The site was converted into a Woolworth's store which closed in 1984. Nowadays it is a car park.

The Myrtle Cinema

1921 Myrtle Cinema.

This was built on Main Street in 1921 on the site of the ancient Hoyle Croft, a grass covered square overlooked by the back of houses on Chapel Lane and Main Street. It had a seating capacity of 900. The cinema provided films twice nightly and also had a matinee.

The first film shown there was *'Alf's Button'* a comedy. In it Leslie Hensen played Alf Higgins, a World War I soldier who discovers that a button on his jacket has unusual magical powers. The late Winifred Harrison in her 1997 book *Days Awake – Childhood Memories of Bingley* captures the atmosphere of that opening film night and the magic of later silent film matinees featuring Lillian Gish and her sister. Lucy Barrett was the local pianist accompanying silent films in the early days.

Top and Bottom

The Myrtle was considered by many Bingley residents to be a little more "posh" than the Hippodrome as it was at the "top" of the town whereas the Hippodrome was at the "bottom".

At the start of films at both the Myrtle and the Hippodrome a news reel would be played which was shared by both cinemas. This involved "runners" from the Hippodrome running up the hill to get the news reel, returning down the hill for the reel to be played and then running back up the hill to return it. Timings at both cinemas had to take account of this requirement.

Bingley College Staff

In *Bingley's Fabulous Fifties - Featuring The Basement Girls* by Joyce Snow (2009), Val Crabtree and Molly Brooke (Sebo), among others, recount their adventures as domestic staff working at Bingley College. Bingley and the local area was their playground as teenagers and as young single women they took full advantage of the Princess and Co-op Halls for dancing and the two cinemas for film going.

Val recalls that after the Coronation in 1953, all the schoolchildren in Bingley went to the Myrtle to see the Coronation in colour and later to see a film capturing the first ascent of Everest.

Coronation Day, Myrtle Cinema on the right.

Rock and Roll

Molly Brooke recounts that she worked as an usherette at the Myrtle in the 1950s, her cinema pedigree enhanced by the fact that her grandmother was manager at the Hippodrome and her father was Manager at the Myrtle.

She remembers the lights going up in the interval and her father playing *Rock Around the Clock* to let teenagers bop to the music in the aisles, one of the few locally to tolerate this. Similar to Mrs Hoyle's musical experience at the Hippodrome 40 years earlier the boppers said that they were not really interested in the films, just being able to bop!

Myrtle Cinema, as it is today.

Eventual Closure

The Myrtle was eventually closed on November 26th, 1960, the last film shown starring the singer Pat Boone in *April Love*. Since then it has been a furniture shop, a Kwik Save and then a Presto Supermarket and in 2000 opened as The Myrtle Grove, a J.D.Weatherspoon's pub. As a building it still retains much of its original shape as an ex-cinema.

End of an Era

The advent of television and other forms of entertainment heralded the demise of local cinema before the transition towards multiplex cinema's located in the centre of cities or on shopping complexes on the outskirts of towns. Perhaps those of us who can remember how cinema once was did not at the time fully appreciate the atmosphere, character and excitement of our visits to the local fleapit!

BINGLEY SWIMMING POOL AND PRINCESS HALL

1927 Opening.

Much has been speculated over recent years about the future of Bingley Swimming Pool. The intention of this chapter is to outline the past history and reasons for building the pool which originally incorporated the Princess Hall for half the year.

Besides my research into the background and history to building both, as part of my ongoing Living History approach during 2012 I interviewed Arthur and Mary Pitchforth who shared some of their memories. These were based on family and work experience of the pool and Princess Hall.

Introduction

From the initial idea of building a swimming pool/public baths in Bingley to such a facility being built took a period of 58 years. The intention of the first part of this chapter is to identify key dates in that development.

First Mention of a Public Baths in Bingley - 1869

At a meeting held in March, 1869, the Bingley Improvement Commissioners stated that they were *"anxious to have public baths situated in the new Prince of Wales Park"*. They were concerned that the river and canal (which had previously been used for bathing and swimming) were "not as pure in water" as they had once been. Additionally, newspaper accounts throughout the 19th Century reported drownings in the canal and the River Aire, of people who could not swim. Consequently, the meeting proposed that baths and a bath house should be built in the park to "accommodate both males and females". The baths were, however, never built and it was to be another 29 years until bathing facilities were built in the centre of Bingley.

Original Public Baths - 1892

The first public baths in the town were opened in the basement of what was then the Library and Town Hall situated in the Mechanics Institute on Main Street. In July, 1892, the Improvement Commissioners adopted the Baths and Washouses Act at a public meeting in Bingley. The sum of £300 was spent in converting the basement of the Mechanics Institute into public baths. The Leeds Mercury of March 12th, 1892, had previously reported *"The erection of **public baths** at Bingley Town Hall is almost completed. There is a Turkish Bath and two first class and five second class slipper baths, each fitted with arrangements for rapid filling and hot water"*.

Only the rich of the period could afford bathing facilities in their houses and the public baths offered the opportunity for a wider range of people to have access to such luxuries. Slipper baths represented the opportunity for people to have an individual and private bath for a relatively small cost.

New Swimming Baths and Princess Hall -1927

In 1926 the whole of the Mechanics Institute was handed over to house Bingley Library and Myrtle Grove then became the town hall. A new **swimming baths and** a public hall called **Princess Hall,** costing £28,000 for the building and equipment

was erected during 1927 on land belonging to Bingley Urban District Council.

E.E.Dodd in his book Bingley (1930:203) stated: *"The long talked about baths were decided upon in 1924. A building was put up at the entrance to Myrtle Park and was opened as the **Princess Hall** by Princess Mary in 1927: the baths were brought into use in the following Spring.* As identified by Dodd, the opening was carried out on **November 24th, 1927,** by HRH Princess Mary, Viscountess Lascelles with her husband, The Earl of Harewood.

The **swimming pool** was opened on **March 12th, 1928** and included exhibitions by Ivy Gill who had swum the English Channel in 1927

Opening.

and by George Webster (appointed an instructor at the pool) who had represented Britain in the 100 metres backstroke at the 1912 and 1920 Olympic Games.

Design of the Facilities

The Council Architect, Eric Robinson, designed the building so that in summer it was used as a **swimming pool** and in the winter a **sectional floor** was installed which covered the pool and provided a dance floor and solid area for functions. This **dance floor** was 80 feet long and 45 feet wide. There was seating accommodation for 762 people (578 in the hall and 184 on the balcony) The Princess Hall was available for events from October to March. During the summer months alternative venues for dancing and functions included the local Cooperative Assembly Hall among others.

The **swimming pool** was 75 feet long and 33 feet wide with a deep end of 6 feet 9 inches and a shallow end of 3 feet 3 inches. The pool also featured three automatic foot sprayers which swimmers had to use before entering the pool, and a number of diving platforms. These consisted of a five metre and a three metre platform and a one metre springboard.

On the evening of the opening an exhibition of high diving and swimming was held at the pool. The facilities also included three slipper baths for children and nine First Class and five Second Class adult slipper baths.

Centre for Electric Therapy and Curative Treatments

In 1925 Bingley UDC was one of the first authorities to provide sun ray facilities in England.

Dr Angus, the local Medical Officer, and J.H.Wright, the Baths Manager, oversaw the introduction of a range of medical, electrical and heat treatments to the new building at Bingley in 1927. Many of these were leading edge innovations for the time.

Additional to sun ray, these included Russian baths and showers, Vichy Douche, Schnee Bath electrical treatment, Radiant Heat cabinets, Diathermy, mud treatments, Bergonic treatments, massage and Pyretic and foam baths.

Examples of Princess Hall Usage

Many patrons of the Princess Hall remember it being used as a dance hall often with live bands and a resident MC. However, the Arts and Community Events also featured heavily in the activities held at the Hall. Opposite are a few examples of these to give a flavour of events:

Year	Organisation	Event
1927	Bingley UDC	Opening Ceremony Dinner Dance
1927	Bingley Primitive Methodists Drama Society	Merrie England Production
1927	Bingley Grammer School	Annual Speech Day in December
1928	Bingley Swiming Club	Whist Drive and Dance
1928	Bingley Primitive Methodists Drama Society	Tom Jones Production
1931	Green Room Players	Amateur Drama
1947	Bingley Little Theatre	The Importance of Being Ernest
1955	Bingley Grammar School	Annual Speech Day in March
1948	Bingley Schools Poetry Competition	Won by Myrtle Park Primary School

Living History

Two local residents, a husband and wife have shared their recollections of Bingley Swimming Pool and the Princess Hall with me, based on their first hand experience and knowledge of the facilities from 1943 to date.

Arthur Pitchforth - Connections to the Pool

Arthur Pitchforth was born in 1943 and initially attended Myrtle Park Primary School.

Arthur's father, Alec William (Bill), was a strong swimmer and water polo player. He represented Great Britain in the 100 yards freestyle at the inaugural YMCA World Games at Copenhagen in Denmark in 1927 and also played water polo against Canada and Sweden.

In 1933 he became a swimming instructor and later a Superintendent at Bingley Swimming Pool and lived at a house attached to the pool which prior to conversion had previously been the stables to Myrtle Grove mansion. His tenure at Bingley was interrupted by war service in the RAF after which he returned to Bingley as a swimming instructor. Arthur was born at the swimming pool house in 1943.

One of Arthur's strong memories is that for health and safety reasons the diving facilities were removed owing to one of the diving platforms being five metres and the pool only two metres at its deep end!

Arthur has held office as President of Bingley Amateur Swimming Club.

Mary Heaton/ Pitchforth

Arthur later married Mary Heaton who worked as a Swimming Instructor at Bingley Pool from 1960 until 2008. Mary was born in Shipley, went to Holy Trinity Primary School and then to the Modern School (now Beckfoot). She met Arthur Pitchforth when he used the swimming pool in his lunch hours. He worked at his mother's hairdressers in Myrtle Place and the pool was near to his work. Mary started work there in 1960.

New Site for the Pool?

Bert Lax, the then Superintendent, prepared a model of a suggested new pool to be sited in the Bottom Meadow at Myrtle Park. The proposal was to have a pool with two shallow ends and a specific diving pool at the side of the main pool. This was considered by Bingley Urban District Council but turned down.

Nothing Was Ever Wasted!

In November, 1960, the Myrtle Cinema in Bingley closed down and a number of five seat rows of gold plush fabric tip-up chairs were bought by the Princess Hall. These were either placed round the edge of the hall when dances were being held or used as main seating in the hall when shows were put on.

Examples of Princess Hall Usage

During the 1960s the pool was closed from the end of October and opened again on March 1st.

Mary remembers the Princess Hall being used for dances on most Saturdays. Many of the local mills held dinners and dances on Fridays there as did NALGO and the Young Farmers. The venue was also used for a Civic Ball each year. An Annual Bingley Week celebration was also held there at which a Miss Bingley was chosen. There were also talent contests held for the annual Bingley Children's Gala. Mary also remembers wrestling being held at Princess Hall but only for one season. Wedding receptions were held in the Solarium. Originally when the Solarium was built, the middle section of the glass windows in the roof were on wheels so that they could be opened.

Millworkers use the Pool

She also remembers that during the 60s and 70s Saturday morning usage of the slipper baths was "manic" and queues back to Myrtle Place would form. Many local millworkers having finished their shift would come straight from work to take their Saturday morning bath.

Medical Treatments

A large number of the treatments offered in the medical facilities in the early years were no longer practised. While J.H.Wright had retired in the mid 1960s as Superintendent, he and his wife still rented rooms and provided some treatment for rheumatism. Mary remembers herself and colleagues being asked to carry out pyretic treatment on customers.

What Happened to the Dance Floor?

The dance floor was made of maple and took ten working days to take up or lay over the swimming pool. All employees were involved in this mammoth task and Mary and colleagues remember large numbers of wood splinters (spells) in their hands as a result of the job. The sprung floor "slotted together like a jigsaw" and was supported on wood beams and trestles laid below it. 1972 was the last year that the floor was laid over the swimming pool. Mary states that the floor was then sold and "Is now all over Bingley", but primarily at Bingley Little Theatre. In 2011 Jeff Peacock, of Bingley Little Theatre, showed me the section of the floor transferred to BLT.

Closure of the Princess Hall Dances

In October, 1972, the venue closed as a public hall and from 1973 was opened as a swimming pool only. Mary attributes the closure to the diminishing number of dances being held in such a large venue. She points towards dances being held in smaller halls such as Eldwick Memorial Hall and the Co-op Hall.

Theatre/The Arts and Community Events and Space

The area in close proximity to the Princess Hall was utilised for community usage: *"Bingley Little Theatre with seats for 150 was in 1974 merged with the Arts Centre. Previously the site of the Oddfellows Hall it was converted in 1948 into a theatre but was compulsorily purchased and demolished in 1974 when the Arts Centre opened – an adjacent building to the Arts Centre formerly a St John's Ambulance Hall was converted to a rehearsal space" (The Theatre Trust 1974).*

Management of the BLT and Arts Centre and running of the facility have also been subject to recent change which was reported in the Bingley Little Theatre Newsletter of June 2012.

The Future of the Swimming Pool

During 2010/2011 speculation that the pool would be closed was rife. A local campaign with over 4,000 signatures and the formation of a local Friends of Bingley Pool in 2015 aims to secure a future for the facility It would be a sad day for Bingley if the 1927 vision and provision by the Bingley Urban District Council should no longer exist.

Thanks to Arthur and Mary Pitchforth and Bradford Leisure Staff at Bingley Pool for their contributions and access/permission to use original photographs. Thanks to Bradford Libraries for permission to use photographs and to Jeff Peacock of Bingley Little Theatre for access to the original swimming pool sectional floor.

EVENTS
QUEEN VICTORIA'S JUBILEE CELEBRATIONS IN BINGLEY

Queen Victoria reigned for 63 years and was honoured by two great public commemorations of her longevity as ruler of the British Empire, namely the Golden Jubilee in June, 1887, and the Diamond Jubilee in June, 1897.

The Golden Jubilee festivities were widely seen not only as a celebration of Queen Victoria but as an affirmation of Britain's place as a global power.

When she reached her 60th anniversary on the throne, Britain marked the occasion with her Diamond Jubilee. The focus of the celebrations were on the growth of the British Empire during Victoria's reign. The 1897 events were distinctive in that they seemed to mark the end of an era as they were the last great gathering of European royalty.

Towns and villages throughout the country organised their own celebrations and commemorations.

Bingley Events
1887

A large public meeting held in Bingley at the Mechanics Institute on February 22nd, 1887, unanimously passed a resolution deciding that *"The memory of the Queen's Jubilee should be perpetuated by the erection of a Technical School and a Cottage Hospital".*

A Jubilee Committee was formed and it was decided that the cost of building both should be by public subscription. Two funds were set up with subscribers deciding which one (or both) to subscribe to. It was also decided to contribute £300, eventually raised on the day, to the Imperial Institute in London.

Harrison (1997) observes that Alfred Sharp, of Bingley, also made a handsome contribution towards the new Technical School.

On June 22nd, 1887, a large procession including Bingley Rifle Volunteers, 5,000 Sunday schoolchildren, 600 members of local friendly societies, the Black Dyke Mills Band and the Bingley Fire Brigade and their engines marched through Main Street to Myrtle Park (then still owned by Alfred Sharp) After a concert in the park local children were treated to a free tea and competed in a number of sports. Around 12,000 people attended the procession.

Dodd (1930) recorded: *"The Queen's Jubilee of 1887 was the occasion for launching two important enterprises, the Cottage Hospital and the Technical School. Apart from the immediate celebration of the event by the inevitable procession (school children, volunteers, Fire Brigade and Friendly Societies) and a concert, a fund of over £3,000 was raised.*

The commemoration of the Diamond Jubilee in 1897 had no such far reaching results. The decorations – triumphal arches and illuminations powered by gas roused great admiration. In the procession hand weavers and wool combers appeared in tableaux as memories of the past".

1897

During the day on June 22nd, 1897, a well attended and colourful parade commemorated both the Queen's Diamond Jubilee and Bingley's loyal service and industrial heritage. In the evening large beacons on the hillsides along the Aire Valley were lit. Speight (1898:281) commented: *"On the night of Her Majesty's Jubilee there was a large gathering of people to witness the huge bonfire blaze on the projection of ground overhanging the valley, about 100 yards south of Druids Altar Rock. There was another large fire at Gilstead Crags on the opposite side of the valley".*

In essence, this celebration heralded the end of an era from a royal perspective. It also signalled a change in the old values and ways of doing things in Bingley as the new century approached.

MILNER FIELD
DROWNING TRAGEDY

Milner Field, the house built by Sir Titus Salt's son, Titus Junior, in the early 1870s, has over the years acquired a reputation for the tragic and early deaths of some of its occupants. Titus Junior died in 1887 aged 44. Later residents, Anne Hollins (43, pneumonia), Arthur Hollins (51, hiccoughed to death), Eva Gates (49) and Ernest Gates (51, septicemia) all died in the period 1923 to 1929.

While not a resident, Tom Mirfield of Manningham, Bradford died an equally tragic death at Milner Field Lake in 1901. This chapter uncovers and looks at a previously long forgotten and little known local tragedy.

Tom Mirfield

Tom Mirfield is shown in the 1901 Census as a Letter Carrier aged 28. He was one of 10 children and had married his wife, Fanny, at St Paul's Church, Manningham on June 12th 1901, only weeks before his death. Besides being a **postman** he was also a **Branch Secretary** of the **Bradford Postmen's Federation**. It seems likely that the postmen held an event at **Milner Field** to raise funds for a strike that the Federation nationally had started in late July, 1901.

Yorkshire Evening Post Report

The newspaper of Tuesday, **August 6th, 1901,** reported the following under the headline *Drowned Unobserved - Fatal Water Polo Game Near Bingley: "Yesterday afternoon a very sad drowning accident took place in the lake of the grounds of Milner Field, near Bingley, the residence of Mrs Titus Salt, during the progress of a Demonstration organised by the Bradford Branch of the Postmen's Federation. The Bradford District includes Shipley and Bingley and fully 200 postmen from the three places, together with wives and lady friends, were in the grounds.*

*The victim was Tom Mirfield (28), postman, of 33, Rose Street, Manningham, who was one of 10 players taking part in a game of **water polo** in the lake".*

The Events

The report then describes the sequence of events. Around 300 spectators had watched the match, which finished at 3.45 pm, from the banks of the lake. On conclusion all but two of the players were thought to have exited the lake via the landing stage. The two who remained in the water then gave a demonstration of what was called "fancy swimming". When their exhibition had finished they went to the area reserved for dressing.

Discovery

The newspaper then states: *"It was found out for the first time that one of the party was missing, in consequence of an **unclaimed set of clothes** being perceived. It was soon established that the clothes belonged to Mirfield and when it was found that he was not anywhere about, fears began to be felt that he had been drowned".*

The Search

A visual search of the lake was then carried out followed by a search using two boats moored on the lake and using oars and poles to probe the water. Failing this it was then decided to run the water off. When the depth of the lake had been lowered enough for people to walk about on the lake bottom a further search was made.

As a result, at about 6.30 pm the body was **found** in the **mud** on the **lake bottom** near the landing stage. The newspaper observed: *"By that time the unfortunate man had been in the water some two hours from when he was actually missed and nearly three hours from the period of the conclusion of the game.*

The Cause

It was thought that the drowning had been caused because Tom Mirfield had suffered **severe stomach cramp** and had been drowned while attempting to get out of the water. The Yorkshire Evening Post concluded: *"He sank without being observed by any of the spectators on account of their attention being absorbed by the exhibition of swimming which was proceeding in another portion of the lake. He had been married about six weeks and the distressing fact was that his wife was present with the spectators. The facts have been reported by the Bingley Police to the Coroner of the district".*

Probate

On August 30th, 1901, probate was granted at Wakefield, records showing that Tom Mirfield of 33, Rose Street, Bradford, had died on August 5th, 1901, at Milner Field Pond in Bingley leaving £167 9s 3d to Fanny Mirfield, his widow.

Tragic Events

Varo (1985) *Shipley Glen Ramble* and Van den Daele and Beale (2011) *Milner Field - The Lost Country House of Titus Salt Junior* make specific comment about tragedy at the Milner Field Estate. Varo observes: *"Since the construction of the New Milner Field in 1872, all the occupants suffered from a tragic series of events, clouding the house with a mysterious and unlucky reputation".*

The drowning described in this chapter and unknown to the majority of people in the local area seems also to be part of a darker side of Milner Field which as a house no longer exists.

Milner Field Mansion.

BOER WAR
COMMEMORATION, 1905

General Rundle Visit to Bingley

On June 3rd, 1905, Major General Sir Leslie Rundle visited Bingley to unveil a memorial for three Bingley soldiers. This had been provided by the public of Bingley in honour of the men who had volunteered for and died in service in South Africa in 1901.

The General was an entirely appropriate choice as he had served and commanded in both the First Boer War in South Africa (1881) and the Second Boer War (1899 to 1902). By the time he visited Bingley in 1905 he was Commander-in-Chief of Northern Command.

The General arrived at Bingley on the 2nd of June and stayed as a guest of William Ferrand at St Ives.

The First Commemoration

There were two commemorations, the first of which was the dedication of a marble tablet memorial in Bingley Parish Church to three soldiers

of the Imperial Yeomanry who had lost their lives in South Africa, namely Privates: Albert Holmes (18) of Fernhill, Lady Lane, Bingley, who died in Pretoria on April 26th, 1901.

Daniel Smith (21) of Bridge Street, Crossflatts, who died in Rhebaksfontein on August 1st, 1901.

Joseph Wild (23) of 8, Raven Street, Bingley, who died in Heilbron on June 10th, 1901.

Church Service

Shortly before 2.30 pm a guard of honour composed of the Bingley (H) Company of the 3rd Volunteer Battalion Duke of Wellington's Regiment marched down Main Street headed by the battalion band and drew up at the principal entrance to the Parish Church. A few minutes later the General arrived with Mr Ferrand. During the service that followed the marble tablet was unveiled by the General and buglers sounded the Last Post.

The Second Commemoration

A brass tablet bearing the names of the 49 men who volunteered from Bingley and District was then to be unveiled at the Town Hall.

Consequently, after the church service the party proceeded to the Town Hall (Mechanics Institute) on Main Street where General Rundle was invited to unveil the brass tablet. This had been commissioned by the Bingley Patriotic Fund and made by Bell and Company, Engravers, of Hall Ings, Bradford. It was made from a solid sheet of brass and included oak leaves and the Bingley Coat of Arms and listed the Yeomanry and active servicemen from the 1899 - 1902 conflict.

The General congratulated all those whose names were on the tablet and *"who had taken part in the defence of the Empire and had returned to their native land"*. The tablet named 38 soldiers from the Yeomanry and 11 Volunteers on Active Service. The tablet read:

1899 – 1902

Bingley Patriotic Fund

This Tablet was erected by the inhabitants of Bingley in recognition of the services given to their country by the under mentioned volunteers from Bingley during the war in South Africa

Presentation of gold commemorative medals

After unveiling the tablet, General Rundle then presented small 22 carat gold medals to each of the men attending, who were named on the tablet, from a raised platform in front of the Town Hall. A new flagstaff was erected in front of the building to mark the occasion.

A Sequel

In 2001, the then Bingley Town Centre Manager, David Dinsey, discovered a dusty plaque in the library the same one that had been unveiled at the old Town Hall in 1905. He assumed that the plaque had been taken down and stored when the old Free Library in the Town Hall closed 40 years before and had it cleaned up to return it to its former glory.

SUFFRAGETTES IN BINGLEY AND AT SHIPLEY GLEN AND WOODHOUSE MOOR, LEEDS

While researching at Keighley Library during 2013 I discovered a long forgotten call to the women of Bingley from an imprisoned Suffragette (who was a local organiser and resident in the town).

A number of events link Bingley and Shipley Glen and Woodhouse Moor, Leeds, as regards Suffragette activity locally. This chapter explores these links and examines in chronological order some of the early Yorkshire connections with the Suffragette movement. My intention is to identify a few of the local people and events that played a part in eventually achieving Votes for Women.

Background
The Suffragettes - Two Active Families

While there were many key players within the Suffrage movement, for the purposes of this article two families who made significant contributions nationally and influenced events locally are identified

The Pankhursts

In October, 1903, Emmeline Pankhurst and her daughters, Christabel, Adela and Sylvia, invited a small group of working-class women, most of them wives of members of the Independent Labour Party (ILP), to their home in Manchester. There they established the Women's Social and Political Union (WSPU), a new form of suffrage group which would essentially change the nature of the movement and surprise the nation with its militant tactics.

The Pankhurst family lived in their Manchester home until 1906 when they moved the operation to London.

The Kenneys

In 1905 Annie Kenney and her sisters, Jessie and Jenny, living in Oldham (and subsequently Springhead, Yorkshire), were invited to a meeting at Oldham Trades Council at which Christabel Pankhurst was one of the main speakers. As a result **Annie** became the first sister to be an active suffragette, eventually becoming a key organiser for the WSPU nationally. Jessie, Jenny and Nell Kenney would soon join their sister as activists.

Annie Kenney and Christabel Pankhurst.

Nell/Nellie (Sarah Ellen **Kenney**) was the third child and eldest sister of the family. Born in Lees near Oldham, she began work as a half-timer in a cotton mill at age 10 but at 24 she left factory work due to ill health and found work in a shop (*Votes for Women* - June 18th 1908). She was so successful in her new job as a shop assistant that her employers put her in charge of two of their shops.

The death of their mother in 1905 is suggested as the point at which the family started to break up.

VOTES FOR WOMEN.

Miss NELLIE KENNEY,
*The Women's Social and Political Union,
4, Clement's Inn, Strand, W.C.*

Nell Kenney - The Bingley Connection

Several reports point towards Nell Kenny then moving to and living and working in Bingley. Nell is identified by the *Evening Post*, April 1907, as a shop assistant of Bingley. Crawford (1999) *The Women's Suffrage Movement - A Reference Guide* identifies that Miss Nellie Kenney of 14, Leonards Place, Bingley, had became the Bingley WSPU Organiser in 1906. Jessie Kenney was also recorded in *Women of the Right Spirit - Paid Organizers of the WPSU (2011)* as in 1906, *"having left factory work to be employed as a secretary in Bingley"*.

The *Keighley Herald* of February 22nd, 1907, records that *"Miss Nellie Kenney the Bingley lady who is at present serving 14 days for her share in the disturbances outside the House of Commons has written to the women of Bingley calling attention to the treatment meted out to the Suffragettes."*

Arrested at the House of Commons

The disturbances referred to were the WSPU march from what was nicknamed the first "Women's Parliament" at Caxton Hall to the

Commons on 13th February, 1907. In the north of England, WSPU organisers had recruited women willing to go to prison in the name of women's suffrage. Nell Kenney and her sisters were among these.

There was a large turnout of women at Caxton Hall. Amid great excitement a resolution condemning the omission of women's suffrage from the King's Speech was passed, as also was a motion that the resolution be taken to the Prime Minister. Then Emmeline Pankhurst's cry `Rise up, women!' was answered by shouts of `Now!' and a procession of about 700 women was formed.

Nell then played a **major part** in the events to that were to follow. The Derby Daily Telegraph of February 14th, 1907, captures the scene:
"Between 5pm and 6pm in the evening the force of suffragettes 700 strong marched out of Caxton Hall singing their war songs as they tramped through the mud. There were two brigades, one headed by Mrs Despart and the other by Miss Nellie Kenney (Bingley), Miss Annie Kenney's sister.

Each brigade was sub-divided into 10 to 12 battalions and each battalion had a leader. Mrs Despart's brigade swung with determined stride down Victoria Street, disorganizing the traffic while Miss Nellie Kenney's brigade took a different route.

The idea of marching to the House of Commons in two brigades was a brilliant piece of strategy, for while the police were trying to stem Mrs Despard's force, the other deployed separately. "When we got to the door of St Stephen's", said Miss Kenney to a Daily News representative, "we were confronted by about a dozen policemen. The door was closed! "You can't come in " said the officer, "You must go back!", "We've come to see the Prime Minister, let us pass", "No you don't", was the reply "and immediately

Annie Kenney being arrested.

137

I was pushed bodily across Old Palace Yard to the iron railing where I had to cling on with both hands to prevent myself from being trampled underfoot by the mounted police. My party was split up in a few minutes I was arrested and marched off to the police station".

While the police attempted to halt the march, the women were determined to make their point. What ensued was a long struggle between mounted police and the suffragettes which continued until late in the evening. By the time the melee ended at 10pm, 51 women, including Nell Kenney, had been arrested and imprisoned for fourteen days. Hence Nell's call for support from the ladies of Bingley!

And then to the South of France!

Extremely resourceful and apparently undaunted by their arrest and imprisonment Nell, along with Mary Gawthorpe, another Yorkshire activist, travelled to France to confront the then Prime Minister only days after their release. Reporting from Paris the Evening Post of April said: *"Misses Nellie Kenney, of Bingley, and Mary Gawthorpe, of Leeds, two of the 51 women's suffragists who were arrested and fined for participating in a disturbance at the House of Commons on 13th February, 1907, interviewed Sir Henry Campbell Bannerman in the dining room of a Cannes train. The Prime Minister tried in vain to dissuade the suffragists from making further demonstrations outside the House of Commons and he refused to introduce a Bill to grant the franchise to women during the current session".*

Full- Time Organiser

In November, 1907, in recognizing her contribution, the WPSU appointed Nell as a full-time organiser where she worked in Northern England, the Midlands and Plymouth, with occasional visits to Scotland to speak at rallies and "at home" talks.

In 1908 Nell was to return to Yorkshire as one of the key speakers at a large rally at Shipley Glen.

Shipley Glen Rally

Local and national newspaper reports of the time identify that between

40,000 and 100,000 people attended a mass rally at Shipley Glen in May, 1908. These reports also state that trains and trams to the Glen were stretched to full capacity.

Stink Bombs

Attention is also given to the fact that gangs of "noisy youths" tried to disrupt speeches given by Suffragette leaders by singing comic songs, shouting, playing tin whistles, ringing bells or releasing sulpharated hydrogen (stink bombs). Accounts suggest that Adela Pankhurst and Mary Gawthorpe *"had the worst time of it. Miss Pankhurst was assailed with eggs and peas but she and Miss Gawthorpe went on to the end, defying their interrupters"*.

Accounts by the Pankhursts

Writing in *Votes for Women* in June, 1908, Adela Pankhurst, who was by then the main organiser in Yorkshire, stated: *"The Shipley Glen demonstration took place on Sunday. It was a great triumph for our cause some 100,000 people gathered round our six platforms. The platforms were arranged as follows:*

1. Mrs E. Pankhurst; Miss Hartland in Chair

*2. **Miss N. Kenney;** Mrs Batchelor in Chair*

3. Miss Mary Gawthorpe; Miss Foster in Chair

4. Miss Lamb; Miss Newton in Chair

5. Mrs Baines; Miss Hartop in Chair

6. Miss A Pankhurst; Miss Massey in Chair

What is clear is that the Suffragette press chose the upper figure of 100,000 attendees figure to stress the success of the rally.

Follow-up article by Emmeline Pankhurst

In *Votes for Women*, (August 27th, 1908) Emmeline Pankhurst gave a more detailed account of the Shipley Glen meeting under the heading of *The Great Votes for Women Demonstration in Shipley Glen, Bradford*. In it she highlights the support received from the people of Bradford, including the City Council: *"For weeks past all Bradford has been talking about the Yorkshire Suffrage Sunday held in Shipley Glen on May 31st. The Tramway Committee made special preparations to convey the extra passengers expected and for some days official notices appeared in all cars announcing the demonstration. The meeting was advertised to begin at 3.30pm, but before noon heavily laden cars began to leave the city and an unending stream of people on foot wended their way to the picturesque glen, the property of the people of Bradford, about three miles away from the city itself.*

When the speakers arrived on the ground, the six platforms were surrounded by dense crowds numbering at least 100,000 people. Never in the history of the glen have so many human beings been gathered together. In the local Liberal Press there had appeared paragraphs suggesting that attempts would be made to disturb the meetings and this suggestion was taken up by small gangs of noisy youths armed with bells and tin trumpets etc.

Nevertheless, the vast audience of orderly and attentive persons prevented any effective disturbance, and at 5 'o' clock a resolution calling upon the Government to enfranchise the women of this country this session was carried with practical unanimity.

When the meeting closed the people would not go away and begged us to hold another meeting in the evening. The Prime Minister expects us to show a popular demand for votes for women. We offer to him the demand of the people of Bradford, which has already spoken officially through its City Council when it adopted some months ago a resolution similar to the one carried at the great open-air meeting on the Suffrage Sunday of Yorkshire".

The Wood house Moor Rally, Leeds

The Pankhurst and Kenney families and Mary Gawthorpe were again in action at another rally attended by a reported 100,000 people at Woodhouse Moor, Leeds, on 26th July, 1908. This was particularly poignant for Mary Gawthorpe who had grown up in the area as a child. The photograph opposite from the Leeds Mercury depicts a scene from the rally.

A Scene on Woodhouse Moor.

On Woodhouse Moor a crowd of some dimensions had gathered either to approve or gratify their curiosity. Our photograph shows Miss Adela Pankhurst addressing the crowd from one platform. The insets are—(1) Mrs. P. Lawrence, (2) Miss Keevil, (3) Mrs. Pankhurst, and (4) Miss Kenney.

Emigration

Having been involved in some of the **early activity** of the Suffragette movement, **Nell Kenney** married a young **journalist** who she had **met at an open-air Suffragette rally** in the **Midlands** in **1908**. She and her new husband **emigrated** to **Canada** in **1909**. Her husband became involved in pioneering work for the employment and training of the disabled.

Mary Gawthorpe continued to **be heavily involved** in the **WSPU** until **1911** when she **retired** due to **ill-health**. In **1916** she **emigrated** to **New York** where she remained **active** in the **American Suffrage movement** and in **Trade Union** activity.

Women and The Vote

Eventually women in the UK were given the vote in **1918** through **The Representation of the People Act** if they were **over 30** and **satisfied certain property qualifications**. In **1928 suffrage was extended to all women over the age of 21** as a result of **The Equal Franchise Act** which became **law** on **July 2nd, 1928. Emmeline Pankhurst** never witnessed this because she **died aged 70** in a nursing home on **June 14th, 1928, 16 days** before the **law** was passed.

GENERAL BOOTH VISITS BINGLEY

Motor Car "Mission"

From the late summer/early autumn of 1904, General William Booth, founder of the Salvation Army in 1865, increasingly used motor transport as a means of touring Britain to spread his message. His first motor tour started in July, 1904, covering Lands End to Aberdeen. In the period between 1904 and 1910 he undertook seven tours of what some nicknamed his motor car "mission".

Prior to this his main means of transport up until the end of the 19th Century had been by the then dominant railway. Booth realised the potential of the motor car in being able to take him where even the railways couldn't. A typical motor tour took four to six weeks and meant that he could traverse the length and breadth of the country with the General stopping to preach several times a day.

Such was the case on July 27th, 1907, when Booth made an afternoon visit to Bingley.

A Civic Welcome - Presentation

The members of Bingley Urban District Council had organised for him to make an address at Bingley as part of a full programme for the day. The Keighley News reported: *"On Wednesday afternoon, General Booth the head of the Salvation Army, paid a brief but memorable visit to Bingley and the town and the public gave a most cordial and stirring welcome to the "grand old man" of that great social and religious organisation. The visit was one of many which the General made to various places on that day, the programme of which was exceptionally heavy, the day's doings forming an item in the motor-car tour which he is at present making".*

He began the day at Skipton and then came to Bingley, arriving just after three o clock in the afternoon. Afterwards he travelled in turn to Shipley, Bradford and Dewsbury, and at each town he was publicly received.

Preparation

Considerable preparations had been made at Bingley for the event. Flags were flying from the Town Hall and many other buildings and lines of streamers had been strung across Main Street at various points. A platform had been erected in Myrtle Place for the Civic Reception with which the District Council decided a few weeks before to honour the General.

The Keighley News reported: *"The afternoon was fine and bright in fact all the conditions were favourable to a successful public function of a unique character for Bingley. The greatness of the public interest was amply proved by the hundreds and thousands present in Main Street and Myrtle Place a considerable time before the distinguished visitor was due to arrive. Not only were there crowds on foot but every point of vantage furnished by the buildings on the line of the route and by those facing onto Myrtle Place was utilised and at Myrtle Place cameras faced the platform from all points.*

Large though the crowd was, however, before half past two 'o' clock it was quickly and very numerously increased from that moment, this being the time that the workpeople came out of the mills and factories and the children were released from school. There seemed to have been something of a general agreement that work and business of all kinds should be suspended for a portion of the afternoon at least. Consequently by a quarter to three 'o' clock – the time the General and his staff were expected to arrive – Myrtle Place, the Main Street above and below and Chapel Lane were all filled with spectators".

Awaiting his Arrival

By this time the seats on the platform had been taken by members of the District Council, clergy and ministers. Mr Rushworth (Chairman) and Mr Platts (Clerk to the UDC) awaited the arrival of the General at the edge of the highway. The appointed time came and passed leaving the sightseers still expectant, but about five minutes to three a hubbub and stir amongst the masses of people announced the arrival of the advance car.

A few minutes later the General's white car arrived, amid tremendous cheering from all sides. He stood up and threw off his travelling coat and then alighted and was presented to Mr Rushworth and Mr Platts with whom he shook hands after which they all proceeded through a space in the crowd which had been kept open to the platform, one of the staff officers holding a sun umbrella over the General all the time.

The Presentation of the Address

The cheering having subsided and something approaching silence having been secured, Mr Platts read the address which had been prepared, the text of which was as follows:-

Bingley Urban District Council

To General Booth

"Sir, The Bingley Urban District Council feel honoured by the opportunity afforded by your visit to Bingley to present to you this address and to record on behalf of the residents of Bingley their hearty appreciation for your life-long and devoted work for the spread of the teachings of Jesus Christ and for the improvement of the submerged portion of the people in all parts of the world.

The proposal to give you a Civic welcome to the town of Bingley, brought forward when it was known that you would be here on this day, was passed by the Council with absolute unanimity, and in the spirit of regard for your noble labours. The Council also trust that you may be spared for many years and be blessed with health and strength to further advance the great and good work in which you have displayed so much interest and ability to the glory of God and to the behalf of the people".

On behalf of Bingley Urban District Council - Samuel Rushworth - Chairman - Town Hall - Bingley July 26th, 1907.

The address was in book form, neatly bound in red morocco leather tooled in gold and surmounted by the Bingley coat of arms.

Immediately Mr Platts had concluded reading the address, Mr Rushworth proceeded on behalf of the Council to present it to General Booth. He then said:

"Unfortunately for us this afternoon General Booth can only stay ten minutes and I am sure we are all most anxious to hear his address".

"I cannot attempt with so little time at my disposal to describe what a worthy man this country of ours has in General Booth. As Chairman of the Bingley Urban District Council it is my privilege and very great pleasure to give to General Booth in your name a most hearty welcome to the town and to say we all hope he may be spared many years to carry on his grand and noble work".

The General's Reply

General Booth, who was greeted with loud cheers as he stepped to the front of the platform, said: *"It would be clearly impossible to for me to make any considerable portion of this immense crowd hear any remarks that I might have been able to offer you and which I should have been glad to offer if there had been the opportunity. I have already spoken at some considerable length this morning and I have three other heavy engagements before the day closes upon me at Dewsbury. When I look at your faces, when I read the welcome you give me written therein in your smiles and in your greeting, when I hear those words spoken, those words read which you have caused to be inscribed upon this address – which I will carry away with me and cherish and care for – and when I hear your words also Mr Chairman, I can only say from the bottom of my heart that I thank you and that I shall carry away with me the memories of this meeting.*

"I rejoice to know that any poor labours of mine have been in any way useful to this important town and I hope as you have expressed this wish sir, that my dear people will go on labouring for the welfare of the poor and the lost and the suffering, who alas, alas are still round about, and I hope that they will go on with a measure of success, and I hope they will go on with the blessing of the people of Bingley.

The General then called upon one of his aides to offer a short prayer at the conclusion of which the General and his staff proceeded to leave the platform.

Short but High Profile

Having arrived late because of his busy schedule, the Civic Presentation had taken approximately 15 minutes from arrival to departure, surely one of the shortest in the history of the town. However, the Urban District Council had achieved its objective of organising a well attended, high profile visit.

It was estimated that during his motor tour of England and Wales at the age of 78 in 1907, General Booth attended 93 receptions, addressed 150,000 people gave 250 interviews and was photographed over 4,000 times.

PEOPLE
MAGNET - THE EARLY DAYS IN BINGLEY

Few people will associate Magnet Trade and Magnet Joinery, recognised national names, with the **humble beginnings** of **Magnet** in **Bingley** in the **early 1900s.** The company has developed and evolved into a well-known brand name, through ups and downs in trade, several recessions, two World Wars, industrial disputes and a number of mergers both within and outside the UK.

This chapter traces the **early days of Magnet** founded by **Tom Duxbury** on **Whitley Street** in **Bingley** up until his death in 1948.

Greengrocers

Thomas or Tom Duxbury was born in Bingley in 1871. His grandfather Thomas had a greengrocer's shop near the Parish Church in the 1850s. His Father, Robert, shown on Tom's Baptism Certificate as a Tin

Plate Worker had by 1881 become a greengrocer living at 15, Princess Street Bingley, with a greengrocer's shop on Mornington Road. Tom followed his father into this business and is shown in the 1891 Census as a greengrocer living with his parents. In 1894 Tom married Sarah Hannah Fox.

In August, 1899, the York Herald announced a testimonial award for gallantry by the Royal Humane Society to: *"Tom Duxbury, Greengrocer, Bingley for plunging into the Leeds Liverpool Canal at Bingley on July 3rd and saving a man who had got into deep water while bathing"*. The 1901 census shows Tom (still a greengrocer) and Sarah living at 6, Whitley Street, Bingley, an address that would become significant throughout the early development of Magnet.

Tom inherited the greengrocer's business from his father who died aged 58 in 1906.

Why Magnet?

Local legend has it that Tom traded **his horse** called **Magnet** to help him buy what was to be called **The Magnet Firelighter Company** based on **Whitley Street.** Later obituary records show that he founded the Firelighter Company in 1906.

In 1907 he sold the greengrocery business at 5, Mornington Road to John and Hannah Hargreaves, the parents of Ellen Hargreaves (who would eventually become his second wife).

From the proceeds of selling the greengrocery shop he built houses known as Magnet Croft on Whitley Street where he and his expanding family lived.

West Yorkshire Electoral Registers and tax returns for the period show Tom living at 6, Whitley Street but also having an interest in houses on Mornington Road and Brunswick Street.

By 1910 the business was becoming larger and more well established in Bingley. The tax returns of that year show that his property interests included a workshop and **stabling** plus a shed and yard on Whitley Street; houses at 4 and 6, Whitley Street and a **Wood Shop** on Whitley Street, which as a business was worth £1,740.

Expanding Family

By the time of the 1911 Census Tom's **occupation** is shown as **firelighter manufacturer** (working at home) and his eldest son Robert is recorded as a firelighter labourer. The family, still living on Whitley Street, comprises Robert (15), Flora (11), Annie (8), Harry Lewis (7), John (4) and Alice (3). In 1911, George Alfred was born. All the sons worked for Magnet at some time with **Harry Lewis** and **John** playing a **significant part** in the later **expansion** of the company.

Tragedy

At age 19 years and eight months Robert, Tom's **eldest son,** signed up as a Private in the Duke of Wellington's 2/6 West Yorkshire Regiment in 1916. On his papers he described his occupation as timber merchant. After training he was eventually posted to France on 5th February, 1917, but was **killed in action** fighting on the Somme within a month of landing, on 2nd March, 1917.

Sarah his mother received a letter on 28th August, 1918, and his remaining personal effects which comprised his cap badge, letters, photos and two cigarette cases. A letter received from the Regiment by his mother on 3rd May, 1919, confirmed the names and ages of his parents, brothers and sisters and grandparents.

Business Continues

Despite personal tragedy for the family, the firelighter business continued with the following advertisements and comment in the Keighley News:

July 2nd, 1917 - Firelight Supplies - *"Phone 136. Firewood 1/6d each. Cardboard Firelighters 2/6 per gross. Magnet Firelighter Co, Whitley Street, Bingley".*

War Waste for Firewood - September 27th, 1919

"Over 300 tons of good sound wood are stacked in the yard of the Magnet Firelighter Company of Bingley. These boxes cost the Government 6s/6d each, but they are now being chopped up for firewood".

Diversification

In **1919** Tom Duxbury set up another company known as The **Magnet Timber and Hardware Company** as a separate entity to the firelighter business. It would appear that initially he bought and sold **Government surplus stock** as advertised in the Yorkshire Post and Leeds Intelligencer of April 11th, 1922.

"Government Surplus – Timbers, spars, posts, rails, tools for all trades, wire netting, corrugated sheets, roofing felt, ladders, barrows, paint, creosote oil: new American lawn mowers 8" to 10" blades 37/6d. Magnet, Bingley".

Additionally he ran a small transport company.

MISCELLANEOUS SALES.

GOVERNMENT SURPLUS—Timber, spars, posts, rails, tools for all trades, wire netting, corrugated sheets, roofing felt, ladders, barrows, paint, creosote oil; new American lawn mowers, 8 and 10 inches blades, 37s. 6d.; 50 Ash Trees, dry, lying at a Leeds siding, 36ft. lengths; £15 the lot.
MAGNET, BINGLEY. Tele. 136.

Selling Off Magnet Firelighting Plant

The decision for Magnet to diversify prompted Tom and his sons **Harry Lewis** and **John** (who had **entered the business in 1920 and 1922**) to consider selling off some of the machinery on the firelighter side of the business. On March 20th, 1922, the following advert appeared in the Yorkshire Post and Leeds Intelligencer:

"Firelighting Plant – three and a half horsepower gas engine, 2 Glovers Open Draft ,Firegrids Machine, Cake Firelighter Machine and Moulds, Rotary Chopping Machine. £30 the lot. Magnet, Bingley".

16 BURLING and MENDING TABLES, 6 Bullets, Perch; £16 16s. the lot.
FIRELIGHTER PLANT, 3½ horse power Gas Engine, 2 Glover's Open Draught, Firegrids Machine, Cake Firelighter Machine and Moulds, Rotary Chopping Machine; £30 the lot.
MAGNET, BINGLEY. Tele. 136.

This was the precursor to eventually selling this side of the business off completely in 1926 (which will be covered later in this chapter).

During this period they also started manufacturing and selling hen huts and fencing. This led to the company eventually making joinery for local builders, a side of the business that continued to grow in the factory on Whitley Street.

Death of Sarah Duxbury

After 30 years of marriage to Tom, **Sarah Duxbury** died aged 51 in **1923**.

Selling off the Firelighting Business

The final sale of the firelighting business and plant was advertised in the Yorkshire Evening Post of January 28th, **1926**: *"Exceptional Opportunity - Plant, Machinery and Goodwill of old established firelighter and firewood business for disposal comprising: super heating vertical boiler – insured 100lb pressure to pass inspections, one 6 horse power electric motor, ball bearing saw bench rising table, complete with shafting and belting, grid, cake and bushing machines and all other accessories, room wanted. Magnet Firelighter Co, Bingley".*

1926 - A Busy Year!

1926 marked the **marriage** of **Tom** to **Ellen Hargreaves** in June of that year. The electoral rolls show them both living at 6, Whitley Street together from 1926 until 1931. Ellen was born in 1889 in Sutton in Craven and in the 1911 Census she is shown as living at 5, Mornington Road with her father, John Hargreaves, a fruit and vegetable Salesman.

Another significant event during **late 1926** was the **further diversification** of Magnet into the **retail joinery** trade by producing door frames, **doors, windows** and **moulding** for local builders. Much of this activity was due to the marketing efforts of Harry Lewis Duxbury and John Duxbury and is demonstrated by an advertisement in the Yorkshire Evening Post of September 23rd, 1926: *"Modern Designs of well furnished doors, moulds and prepared work made from selected red wood, get our **1926 catalogue and save money**. Magnet Co, Bingley".*

1926 to 1928

The renamed **Magnet Company** founded by Tom Duxbury and his two sons was launched in 1927 and having found a gap in the market was by 1928 supplying components for houses being built throughout the UK.

Phillip Thomas Duxbury, son of Tom and Ellen, was born on September 4th, **1928**.

1929 to 1930

The Keighley News of March 2nd, **1929,** announced a **major fire** at Magnet's Timber Yard Works on Whitley Street, which could have ended the business. The blaze was discovered at about 10pm by **George** Duxbury, **Tom's youngest son,** who saw flames leaping out of the roof of the building, from his bedroom window. Despite their efforts the fire brigade was unable to save the machine shop and several large stacks of timber stored in the yard. The newspaper reported that the firm was exceptionally busy.

The fire resulted in the factory having to be rebuilt and the machinery lost in the fire needing to be replaced or updated. Ellen Duxbury sold two houses to help finance this by loaning Magnet the money. John Pickles, of Hebden Bridge, and Hewitt and Stringer (Timber Merchants), Hull, also helped.

In the event only one contract was lost and the firm was back in production within six weeks of the fire.

Andrew Michael Duxbury, son of Tom and Ellen Duxbury, was born January 18th, **1930**. Both he and Phillip his brother would, like their half-brothers, have a significant contribution to make to the future development and expansion of Magnet.

Move From Whitley Street - 1932

From 1926 until 1931 Tom and Ellen are shown on the electoral registers as living at 6, Whitley Street, an address long occupied by the Duxbury family. In 1932 Land Registry records show them buying land and a building on Street Lane, Morton. Electoral rolls from 1932 until 1948 show them living at High Point, East Morton.

Joint Service Agreements - 1936

In March **1936** Tom Duxbury announced that he was entering into Joint Service Agreements with his sons, Harry Lewis and John, for a period of seven years from March 1st, 1936, at a salary of £1,750 each. Shares were to be allocated as follows:

Tom Duxbury, 1668 shares; Harry Lewis Duxbury, 1666 shares; John Duxbury, 1666 shares.

He further announced: *"My sons who have been associated with me for many years are continuing to be actively engaged in the business of the company and have entered into service agreements as Joint Managing Directors".*

Selling Shares in Magnet on the Stock Market - 1936

The Times of July 3rd, 1936, gave details of the company's intention to become a public limited company.

The heading read: *"Application is made on Friday 3rd July 1936 for permission to deal in shares for Magnet Joinery Ltd. Directors Tom Duxbury, Chairman, East Morton, Harry Lewis Duxbury, Bingley, Joint Managing Director, John Duxbury, Bingley, Joint Managing Director.*

Tom Duxbury stated: "The Magnet Company Limited was formed in 1927 for the purpose of acquiring the business founded by me in 1919 and known as the Magnet Timber and Hardware Company. The business, which has expanded progressively, consists of the production of moulded woodwork and standard joinery which is supplied to all parts of the country. The company owns moulding mills and joinery works at Whitley Street, Bingley, fronting the Leeds and Liverpool Canal and connected with the LMS railway sidings by overhead conveyors.

In close proximity to these works the company rents a flour warehouse at Airebank Mills and owns freehold property of over two acres at Healey Lane, Bingley, with a frontage to the LMS railway main line, both these properties being used for additional storage purposes".

In launching the company on the Stock Market, Tom Duxbury declared *"Gentlemen in response to your request I have pleasure in giving you the following information regarding Magnet Joinery Ltd".*

This included the Surveyors and Valuers Report prepared by Fuller, Horsey Sons and, Cassell which stated: *"The works are equipped with modern plant specially selected for the economical production of builders joinery of every description, each machine being either motorised or individually motor driven and the organisation leaves nothing to be desired".*

1937 to 1939

In 1937 it was decided to build a factory in Grays, Essex, close to the River Thames with the intention of making and selling joinery in the south. Five acres of land was bought in August, 1937, and a new factory built.

Shareholders meetings in the lead up to World War II reported that Magnet had become one of the largest manufacturers of wooden windows and stormproof windows in the UK. Yearly dividends showed an upward increase during this period with increasing returns for shareholders.

1940 to 1946

All appeared to be going well until the start of World War II when from September, 1939, orders dried up. A saving grace was that Magnet received Government orders for Nissen Huts and ammunition boxes to supplement lost business. Many male employees were called up and the firm employed local women to keep production going.

In March, 1942, Tom Duxbury bought a sawmill in Knaresborough to supply the firm with home grown timber, import of timber at the time being difficult.

Tom Duxbury reported that in supporting the war effort from 1940 onwards, Magnet had: *"Produced wooden components for Nissen Huts and hospitals in every area of the world. Magnet has also made wooden tables, windows and camp fitments and ammunition boxes and smoke generator crates by the millions. At the same time doors and windows have been produced for blitzed areas of the country and parts for prefabricated houses have also been manufactured".*

In December, 1946, the Government decided that to save fuel deliveries would be restricted to within 100 miles of any factory. For Magnet this potentially cut off Birmingham and the Midlands, one of their best markets. It was therefore decided to open a factory at Love Lane, Aston, Birmingham.

Deaths

Harry Lewis Duxbury died at home of a heart attack in February, **1943,** at the age of 38, having purchased West Riddlesden Hall only the year before.

Tom Duxbury in his garden at High Point, Morton.

Tom Duxbury died in February, **1948,** at the age of 76. An **Obituary** of the time recorded: *"We regret to record the death which occurred on February 5th of Mr Tom Duxbury of High Point, Morton. Mr Duxbury, in early life a greengrocer was founder of Magnet Firelighter Company in 1906. The concern developed into the firm of Magnet Joinery and with the assistance of his two sons has been built up into the large public company of prepared joinery manufacturers.*

Always willing to help a deserving cause, Mr Duxbury devoted half a century to religious work. For more than 30 years he was an active worker at Bingley Baptist Church and was prominently identified with the old Baptist Dubb Mission. In recent years he had attended Morton Congregational Church.

Twice married, he leaves a widow, four sons and three daughters".

Thanks to Stephen Duxbury for factual content and for permission to use photographs from his collection in this chapter.

MURIEL AKED

From Mill Owner's Daughter to Stage Actress and Film Star

The history and demise of Bingley's two main cinemas is explored on pages 106-111 This chapter traces the background to **Muriel Aked,** of Bingley, who became a renowned **stage and film actress** over the period 1916 to 1953. It is entirely possible that Bingley cinema goers watched the Bingley actress at the town's Hippodrome and Myrtle cinemas during this period!

Muriel appeared in over 40 sound films as a character actress usually portraying maids, spinsters, aristocratic ladies or dowagers. Her talents as a comedienne and occasional Shakespearean actress on stage and radio were also widely recognised.

Bingley Roots

Muriel Aked was born in Bingley on November 11th, 1883, as the daughter of George Henry Aked, a mill owner, and his wife, Emma (nee Bairstow). Her father was originally a founder of Botany Mills, Morton, and latterly a partner in Airedale Mills, Bingley. Later in his life he became Chairman of Bingley Urban District Council. The house in which the family lived is now the Five Rise Hotel, Bingley.

Education in Bingley but Links to Saltaire

George Aked chose a private education for his children and the 1901

Census shows that at age 17 Muriel and two of her sisters, Olive and Georgie, were pupil boarders at **Caldecote Towers in Bushey Heath,** Hertfordshire which had been opened as a Ladies Private School in 1891.

But why Caldecote?

The owner and founder of the school was **Medina Sarah Griffith** who had originally been appointed by **Sir Titus Salt** as the first Headmistress of the **Girls High School in Saltaire in 1876** and who had established an excellent reputation. She moved from Yorkshire as she found the climate to be inclement. A contemporary commentator observed: *"In the beautiful grounds of Caldecote Towers to which she moved in later years, Medina delighted in producing outdoor pageants, tableaux and Shakespearean Dramas".* The 1901 Census shows that at the time the Aked sisters attended the school, Medina aged 61 was School Mistress.

It is highly possible that George Aked chose Caldecote for his

Caldecote Towers.

daughters because he knew of Medina's reputation while at Saltaire and that Muriel's interest in acting was also stimulated and nurtured during her time at the school. Muriel returned to live in Bushey from 1936 to 1953 so the location obviously had resonance for her.

1911 to 1915 Bingley

The 1911 Census shows Muriel as a lady of "own means" to be living in Bingley with her mother, her father having died in 1906. The *World Film Encyclopaedia (1993)* identifies that for a number of years she gained experience by performing successfully in amateur theatricals before her first professional experience in Liverpool.

Stage
1916 to 1920

She initially entered the theatre as a student at **Liverpool Repertory** for six months before making her first appearance there as a nurse in *Alice Sit by the Fire.* The Stage Year Book 1916 shows that in March 1916 she appeared *in Hush,* a comedy in three parts. Advertised in the book was advice on Theatrical Touring in the Far East and it would seem that this stirred her interest because in 1920 she **toured the Far East** with Edgar Warwick's English Comedy Company.

Touring Abroad

In August, 1920, she and 10 other members of the company, including Edgar Warwick, their Theatrical Manager, sailed to Colombo. Newspaper archives show that the tour of theatres covered Ceylon (now Sri Lanka) India, Singapore and China (Shanghai). Departure records show that in May, 1921, Muriel (identified as an actress) returned to London from Bombay as a first class passenger aboard the RMS Mandola.

1920 to 1930

She made her first appearance on the London stage as the Woodcutter's Wife in the Roses and the Ring at Wyndhams Theatre in December **1923**. She worked during this period mainly as a stage actress but also appeared in two silent films A Sister to Assist Er (**1922**) and Bindles Cocktail (1926).

During the 1920s and up until 1930 she performed at the Kingsway Theatre, Arts Club Theatre, Garrick, Lyric and Aldwych Theatres in London. She made her first stage appearance with John Gielgud (later to be Sir John Gielgud) in Prejudice (1928) and in the same year was one of the three witches in Macbeth at the Royal Court Theatre.

1930 to 1939

Opposite are a sample of the films Muriel appeared in during the period and the lead actors/actresses she appeared with. Her full film and stage bibliography can be found on www.britishsites.co.uk/theatre/actors/muriel aked. While still acting on the stage, she concentrated primarily on her film career which gained momentum as the decade progressed.

Goodnight Vienna	**1932**	Anna Neagle, Jack Buchanan
No Funny Business	**1933**	Gertrude Lawrence, Laurence Olivier
The Good Companions	**1933**	Jessie Matthews, John Gielgud
Friday the 13th	**1933**	Jessie Matthews, Max Miller
Autumn Crocus	**1934**	Ivor Novello, Jack Hawkins
Evensong	**1934**	Evelyn Laye, Alec Guiness
Can You Hear Me Mother?	**1935**	Sandy Powell
The Secret Battle	**1939**	Rex Harrison, Valerie Hobson
A Girl Must Live	**1939**	Margaret Lockwood, Renee Houston

1940 to 1953

Muriel became an established part of the British film scene during this period while also continuing to act on stage. In the mid 1940s she appeared on radio in a number of Shakespearean plays. The last film of her career was The Story of Gilbert and Sullivan in which she played Queen Victoria.

Film	Year	Lead Actor/Actress
Kipps	1941	Michael Redgrave, Phyllis Calvert
Cottage to Let	1942	John Mills, Alastair Sim, George Cole
The Demi-Paradise	1943	Laurence Olivier, Margaret Rutherford, Joyce Grenfell
2000 Women	1944	Flora Robson, Dulcie Gray, Renee Houston, Thora Hird
The Wicked Lady	1945	Margaret Lockwood, James Mason
The Years Between	1946	Michael Redgrave, Flora Robson, Valerie Hobson, Dulcie Gray
So Evil My Love	1948	Ann Todd, Ray Milland, Moira Lister, Stanley Holloway, Richard Todd, Glynis Johns
The Blue Lamp	1950	Jack Warner, Tessie O'Shea, Dirk Bogarde, Alastair Sim, Margaret Rutherford, Joyce Grenfell
The Story of Gilbert and Sullivan	1953	Robert Morley, Peter Finch, Wilfred Hyde White

Margaret Rutherford and Muriel Aked.

Film and Stage Critic Quotes

As testament to her undoubted talent, below are just a few examples of the of the critical acclaim Muriel achieved across four decades:

1923   *Muriel Aked has only to speak for a responsive roar to sound from the audience*

1926   *Muriel Aked as Mrs Hellwith was so good I held it not to be acting at all*

1930   *The incomparable Muriel Aked has only to open her mouth to create storms of laughter*

1942   *The unforgettable Muriel Aked purveyed her customary essence of aunthood*

1953   *John Gielgud in his book Early Stages remembers the film drama Friday the Thirteenth in which "Ralph Richardson played a small part beautifully and Muriel Aked was brilliant"*

And Finally.....

In 1953 Muriel sold her home in Bushey to return to Yorkshire where her sister, Olive, lived in Settle. On 21st March, 1955, Muriel Aked died after a long and illustrious acting career, at her home, **Bushey**, Ingfield Road, Settle at the age of 67.

Muriel as Queen Victoria 1953 in her last film.

SIR FRED HOYLE – CHILDHOOD DAYS IN BINGLEY AND GILSTEAD

This chapter traces the early childhood of **Fred Hoyle,** born in **Gilstead** in **1915,** and identifies some of the **educational events** which shaped him while growing up in the local area. Contributions and observations are made within the Chapter by Fred's son Geoff Hoyle.

Sir Fred Hoyle Way

In 2009 local councillors successfully led an appeal to get part of the Bingley Relief Road

renamed to recognise the career of Sir Fred Hoyle. Sir Fred Hoyle Way now marks the stretch of road between Crossflatts and Cottingley.

His Career

Fred Hoyle was, among other notable achievements, an **Academic, Mathematician, Astrophysicist Astronomer, Cosmologist, Broadcaster and Science Fiction Writer** who coined the phrase **Big Bang Theory** then rejected it in favour of **Steady State Theory. Controversial** and **forthright,** he was known throughout his career for his **independence of mind** and as a lifelong rebel **eager for intellectual combat**. He was Knighted in 1972.

His Parents

Fred's **mother** was **Mabel Pickard** who despite her own father William, a Quarry Foreman, dying in his early 30s, managed her own education and finances extremely well. Initially starting work in a Bingley mill as a worsted coating mender she gained a further education qualification which got her a place at the **Royal Academy of Music** where she first studied singing, then piano. After this she started to teach music and the 1911 Census shows her aged 30 working as an elementary **school teacher** for a County Council in East Yorkshire.

The year before she had bought two adjoining two bedroom properties at Milnerfield Villas (now Primrose Lane) which had previously been accommodation for high ranking domestic and gardening staff working on the Milner Field Estate. In 1911 Mabel married her first cousin, **Ben Hoyle**.

Ben had left school at 11 in 1893 to work in a mill. He was the **great grandson of Ben Preston** the well-known Yorkshire Dialect Poet who lived in Gilstead. At age 22 Ben emigrated to the USA with his brother George. Fred's son, Geoff Hoyle informs me the reason for this was that Ben mistakenly thought that he had killed someone in a pub fight. During his time in America the Hoyle family think that he worked his way down the eastern sea board and ended up picking bananas on one of the Caribbean Islands, possibly off Cuba.

Ben returned in 1906 to help support his widowed mother. The 1911 Census shows him working as a **Rag and Fent Merchant,** as an **employer** and living with his mother at 14, Adelaide Street, Bingley. He and Mabel **married** in Autumn, **1911**.

Geoff Hoyle observes: *"As was the custom at the time Mabel had to relinquish her teaching post on marriage. (My father's support of women probably came from this treatment of his mother.) The most notable instance was in 1975 when my father commented that Jocelyn Bell should have been honoured along with other recipients of the Nobel Prize for the discovery of Pulsars".*

War Years

Fred Hoyle was born on June 24th, **1915,** and Ben, his father, was conscripted in the same year. Ben eventually served in the newly formed **Machine Gun Corps** and by a mixture of guile and good luck managed to survive the war in what was an extremely dangerous occupation.

Mabel, in the meantime, eked out a living on the one shilling a week she received for being the wife of a serving soldier. She supplemented her income by using her undoubted musical talent by **playing piano** to accompany silent films in the evening at the **Hippodrome Cinema**, Main Street, **Bingley**.

Fred's Early Learning

Fred was lucky in having parents who themselves had **not taken the traditional route** to formal **learning** and who encouraged him to **be inquisitive**. While his mother was at home during the day she could devote time to looking after him (he was regarded as a "delicate" child) whil also **facilitating his learning**. As such he could transcribe and recite his multiplication tables and read the time on a clock face by the age of four. He was also fascinated by machines and recalls in his book *The Small World of Fred Hoyle (1986:27)* how in **1918** worried neighbours called his mother to collect him after he had stood mesmerised for two hours watching a steamroller mend potholes in the road through Gilstead.

Consequently on returning home from World War I in **1919**, Ben Hoyle found his son well **advanced** in **numbers** and with an avid **interest** in **all things around him.** Fred himself later wrote however that it was **not until** he was age seven that he **could read**. This occurred when he found that he could suddenly read the subtitles to silent films at the cinema without difficulty.

Boom to Bust

By **1920** Ben Hoyle had set up a cloth business in Bradford which at first rode the wave of a trade boom, exporting goods as far as China. Dividend records for June, 1920, also show that he traded as Metcalf and Hoyle from Ebor Mills, Dubb Lane, Bingley and was living at Milnerfield Villas, Bingley.

At first the business flourished and as a result of having some surplus income Ben and Mabel decided to send Fred to a small private Dame School situated near what is now Damart. However, there was a general slump in business in 1921 and Fred only attended the school for a week in July, 1921. Allied to the slump, family factors, namely the birth of the couple's second child, Joan, and the serious illness of Mabel caused the family to move temporarily to Rayleigh in Essex. They rented one of their houses in Bingley out as a result.

Truancy then Return to Bingley

After the summer holiday Fred enrolled at the local village school in Thundersley, Essex, where he and another boy, Freddie Clamp worked out a truancy system which meant that neither of them spent much time at the school. Fred later recalled: *"This system supplied the essential basis of the technique I was to use in succeeding years"* (Hoyle, 1986:54).

1921 Thundersley School Essex.

Fred's family returned to Gilstead in November, 1921, on hearing that there were problems with the people to who had rented their house and had done a "flit" leaving Ben Hoyle to settle their debts. Back home, Fred was returned school in January 1922: *"I returned to the same private school as before but I returned no longer an innocent child prepared to have irrelevant knowledge poured into my head by the old dame who ran the place"* (Hoyle, 1994:44).

Truancy and Illness

Fred lasted at the school until March, 1922, when unimpressed with the teaching he put into practice the truancy skills he had employed while in Essex. Persuading his parents that he was going to school and asking a friend to tell school that he was ill, he managed to **evade school** until this ruse was found out in May. His parents then explained the **law governing attendance at school** and the **repercussions** of non attendance on the family and gave him the option to choose a new school.

He chose **Mornington Road School** where he started in September, **1922,** having already missed a considerable amount of his early education. Fred appears to have **suffered** school but found a temporary escape during the winter and early of 1923/24 through **illness**. He later stated: *"By now I had learned that illness was the key to absence. Doubtless I experienced some genuine illness during the winter of 1923/24 but additionally I spun out every small sniffle into a week or ten days".* *Eventually he had his tonsils removed and he managed to "stretch the convalescence to two months"* (Hoyle, 1994:48).

Fred returned to school in the Spring term but then had a difference of opinion with a teacher who then hit him. He immediately left the school premises, went home and informed his mother that he was *"finished with school".* Despite an attempt at compromise between Fred's mother and the school and a meeting with the local education committee he still managed to convince his parents that he was attending school.

Observational Learning

Despite his attempts to avoid the formal education system, Fred did show interest in **educating himself** through taking a **pragmatic** approach to learning new things. Appearing to go to school he instead spent time **visiting local factories** and **workshops** and **asking questions** of the workers that he was **observing**. Returning to Gilstead with his father in 1997, Geoff recalls his father describing the noise from the mills as deafening. *"He used to walk into Bingley from Gilstead and once he started down Ferncliffe Road the noise increased with each step, particularly on a still day. A windy day helped disperse the noise. On occasions he went* *into the mills to observe the working of machines and found the noise even more deafening".*

He also spent many hours at **Five Rise Locks** watching the simple engineering ingenuity of the operation of the lock gates and sluices. Later in life he would attribute an early interest in hydraulics and mechanics to the observations he made during this period. Geoff comments *"He would also walk the canal while playing truant and count the dead dogs in the canal. He would also see the canal being cleaned of these poor creatures every so often".*

In contrast, in the afternoons he often spent time **watching** and **studying natur**e, flora and fauna, on the moors and in the woods before returning home as if he had been to school. Throughout his life he enjoyed the outdoors, particularly fell walking.

Initially too young to have a ticket to Bingley Library, Fred searched his father's small **book collection** and found an introductory text book on **chemistry**. He also discovered equipment which his father had bought in his youth such as flasks, corks, retorts and a Bunsen burner and several bottles of reagents. On reading the book he identified the additional equipment and solutions needed to carry out **experiments** and then caught the tram into Bradford to buy these at a **chemist's shop** in Sunbridge Road. Experiments from the book were then carried out in the kitchen of number 34 and Fred particularly enjoyed those involving explosions and bad smells!" Through this formative experimentation he found an interest in the subject that would last a lifetime.

A notable visit to an Easter Fair at Shipley Glen in 1923 resulted in Ben Hoyle paying to watch a wireless demonstration. As a result he and Fred bought and collected components and connections and **built** their own **wireless**.

Fred's **inquisitive** and **enquiring nature** made him a **willing** and avid **learner** by non traditional routes. In later years he would recall: *"Between the ages of five and nine I was perpetually at war with the educational system. My father always deferred to my mother's judgement in the several crises of my early educational career, because she had been a schoolteacher herself ... events would suggest that my mother was unreasonably tolerant* *of my obduracy. But, precisely because she had been a teacher herself, my mother could see that **I made the best steps when I was left alone**".* (Hoyle, 1994:42).

A Third School and then a Scholarship

Despite Fred's **chequered educational career**, his parents were determined that he would win a **scholarship** to **Bingley Grammar School** at age 11. Consequently he moved to Eldwick School in **September, 1924,** aware that the West Riding Educational Authorities only awarded about a dozen such scholarships in the Bingley area each year.

Part of the rationale for sitting the scholarship was based on the fact that Fred's father had won such a scholarship but had not been able to take it up. Through the death of his own father, Ben Hoyle had been required to go out to work and earn a wage to support his widowed mother and young brother. Fred's view was: *"There seems to have been an almost compulsive wish to compensate for things in my own generation".* (Hoyle, 1994:56). Another plus for the school was that Tommy Murgatroyd, the headteacher, had previously been a teaching colleague of Mabel Hoyle.

Starting in the Junior classroom Fred graduated to the Senior ranks of the school by January, 1925, and from there on worked his way up the academic pecking order.

For Christmas, 1925, his parents bought him a brass refracting **telescope** which they purchased from Clarksons Optical Stores in London. This started a **lifelong interest** in the stars and constellations which would stand him in good stead in his **future career** as an academic. His telescope was donated by his family to Cambridge University and now forms part of an online exhibition of his papers and personal effects. (www.joh.cam.ac.uk/library/special_collections/hoyle/exhibition/telescope).

In February, 1926, he took the **West Riding County Minor Scholarship Examination**. Winning a scholarship entitled entrants to attend their nearest Grammar School. Despite not passing the examination, because only half the usual number of scholarships were awarded to the Bingley area, Fred was invited back for interview with Alan Smailes the headteacher, who was a graduate of the Mathematical Tripos at Cambridge. He must have impressed Smailes, and Herbert Haigh, the chemistry teacher, with his account of his chemistry book experiments and knowledge of the stars because he was **awarded a scholarship** to the school.

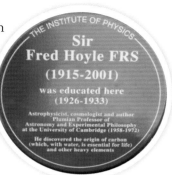

Bingley Grammar School

Photo: Mark Hurn.

Fred started Bingley Grammar School in September, 1926. His war with the education system apparently at an end he proved to be an avid reader and systematic learner. By now a regular user of Bingley Library, in 1927 he acquired a copy of Eddingtons *Stars and Atoms* which along with his telescope further germinated his interest in astronomy.

Starting the school as 16th out of a class of 32 he progressed to fifth, second then first in his first year. During his second and third years he was always in the top three in the class. In his fourth year and aged just 15 he took and passed his **Matriculation Examinations** and returned to study for his Higher Certificate.

University Entrance Exams
Leeds

Mentored by Alan Smailes, Fred set his sights on gaining a **County Major Scholarship** to support him at university where he hoped to study chemistry at Leeds. He passed his **Higher Certificate** and took the Scholarship examinations in 1932, attaining the previously accepted standard. However, due to education cuts during the Great Depression, Yorkshire raised its standards and he did not receive an award.

Cambridge

Unable to attend university without a Scholarship, Fred returned to Bingley Grammar. To gain a place at Leeds and make a second attempt at doing so he would have to repeat a year. Unhappy with this he

171

sought Smaile's advice and decided to try for a Cambridge University Scholarship instead.

Fred sat the examinations at **Emmanuel College** in December, **1932.** In a reference to Emmanuel College, Smailes wrote: *'I certainly believe he will turn out to be a 'swan', no matter what sort of duckling or gosling he now appears'.*

Although performing well in physics and chemistry he missed the exhibition standard that he needed for entrance. Undaunted, he crammed for the examinations at **Pembroke College** in March, **1933,** with the assistance of Smailes and Haigh. This time he made the exhibition standard. Unfortunately, the college did not have scholarships for everybody achieving the standard and again he missed out.

However, he could now get into Cambridge by winning a scholarship and funding in the forthcoming **Yorkshire Scholarship** competition. He achieved this in the **summer of 1933** with **mathematics** being his best subject. He entered Emmanuel College in **October, 1933,** and was advised by his tutor to study mathematics with funding from **West Yorkshire County Council**.

And Then...

The intention of this chapter has been to cover Fred Hoyle's **childhood** in **Bingley** and his **self-made approach** to education, even at a **young age**.

His **Academic** career was **no different** in terms of the way he continued to **challenge** and debate accepted norms and theories. The Complete Dictionary of Scientific Biography (2008) identifies how **the circle began once again once** he started at university....

"From the moment he arrived in Cambridge, in October 1933, Hoyle was an outsider. His impoverished background, old clothes, and marked regional accent set him apart from the polished members of the aristocracy and the privileged elite from England's major private schools. He immersed himself in his studies with stunning success. The university graded him first class at the end of his freshman year. He skipped the second-year curriculum entirely, and moved onto graduate-level courses for his third year. He graduated as the top-ranked applied mathematician of his year".

Fred was obviously doing what he was best at. Just being Fred!

Jane Gregory (2005), one of his biographers, captures the essence of Fred Hoyle and his approach to life in describing him as *"A down-to-earth Yorkshireman who combined a brilliant scientific mind with a relish for communication and controversy".*

Evidence of his interest not only in academic matters but also in sport and his local roots, is shown by the fact that as a native-born Yorkshireman, Fred had a lifelong interest in cricket. A photograph (below) supplied by Geoff Hoyle, Courtesy of The Master and Fellows of St John's College, Cambridge, captures Fred practising with his cricket bat as a young boy in Bingley. Geoff also recalls that as a boy he was taken by his grandfather Ben, also a cricket fan, to see another Fred, namely Fred Truman playing on a cricket pitch near Salts Mill.

Thanks to Geoff Hoyle, for his observations and factual content as regards information about his father in this chapter.

SECTION FOUR
BINGLEY'S TOWN CRIER – A FAMILY REMEMBERED

During 2014 Bingley Hub reader Sue Brown (nee Green) contacted me to share the background of her family as Town Criers of Bingley.

This chapter is the result of our meetings to discuss the contributions her family has made and my further research.

BINGLEY BELLMAN.

OLD PAINTING AS CLUE TO EARLY OFFICE-HOLDER.

As the result of a paragraph which appeared in the "Telegraph and Argus" recently concerning the appointment of Mr. Ben Green, of Bingley, as the town's bellman, information has come to light which establishes the name of the man who held the office before Mr. Green's grandfather was elected town crier in 1853.

He was John Crowther, of Slicer Yard, Bingley, and evidence in support of this is provided by an old painting depicting Mr. Crowther, who is wearing a frock-coat and top hat,

with a bell under his arm. Mr. Crowther's grand-daughter told a "Telegraph and Argus" reporter that in addition to carrying out his duties as bellman, Mr. Crowther used to act as the town's official knocker-up.

"PIKE AND RATTLE."

Reference to Mr. Crowther is made by the late Mr. Harry Speight in his book "Bingley and District." Mr. Speight states that Crowther acted as assistant parish constable, and also as night watchman.

"He paraded the streets at all hours of the night," writes Mr. Speight, "armed with pike and rattle, and cried the hour and state of the weather."

The office of bellman has been in the Green family for nearly 80 years, Mr. W. Green, who died a week or so ago, succeeding his father, the late Mr. J. Green, in 1873. Mr. W. Green held office until four years ago.

Three Generations of Town Crier

Joseph (Joe) Green, born in 1803, served Bingley at first as Parish Constable initially appointed by the Vestry (a body responsible for the affairs of a Parish). In 1853 he was appointed pinder (receiving a small fee for every stray animal impounded) and bellman (paid for every announcement made). As such Joe was the first official Town Crier, appointed by the Keighley Court, acting as Court Leet, (who made such bellman appointments), in 1853 and in 1872.

Joe is shown in the Census of 1851 as Parish Constable and the Census of 1861 as Town Crier.

Prior to this John Crowther, (although not Town Crier), had paraded Bingley throughout the night armed with a pike and a rattle and cried out the hour and state of the weather in his role as the Town Knocker Up. An old oil painting (shown in newspaper cutting, opposite) depicts Crowther wearing a frock-coat with a bell under his arm. This was one of two bells used by the town during this period.

TOWN CRIE OUT OF WORK

But The Tradition Lives On

From Our Special Corresponde

BINGLEY, Yorkshire.

The noisest job in Bingley h become the quietest, according Ben Green, Bingley's town crie for nobody has anything to " cry these days.

But Ben means to keep up the o custom of town-crying in Aireda just the same. With him it is a que tion of family tradition.

The office, now almost extinct for a practical purposes, has not been ou of the Green family for three genera tions. It was held by Ben's gran father in 1853. Then it was passed o to Ben's father, who held the post fo 60 years and never once missed " cry ing " the classes at the Airedale Show for half a century.

Then old Bill Green died, but he saw his son as his successor handing over the famous hand-bell which has heralded the shouting of news in the streets of Bingley for generations.

A FAMOUS BELL

The bell is one of Ben's proudest possessions. Even Mrs. Ben dare not handle it and Ben himself polishes it until he can see himself in it.

" Town-crying is not what it was," he told me. " I've only had two jobs since I began, but we are going to keep the idea alive."

And despite the fact that there are no calls in these days, Ben has his eye on his son Stanley. " Before he's 21 I shall take him round with me—that is, if there's anything to go round for," he says.

BINGLEY TOWN CRIER.

Son Succeeds His Father.

Although there is little demand upon the services of any North of England town crier nowadays the office is still being carried on at Bingley.

Mr. William Green, who died last week, held the office for more than 50 years, but four years ago, owing to indisposition, he expressed the wish that his son, Mr. Ben Green, of Crow Nest Lane, Bingley, should carry on in his place, and his son acceded.

The office of town crier at Bingley has been in the Green family since 1853, the present holder's grandfather being the first bellman for the town, and following his retirement from the position in 1872 his son, the late Mr. William Green, was appointed at a court leet when the Lord of the Manor was Mr. George Lane Fox.

RARELY NEEDED NOW.

During this period two bells have been used, the original having to be recast soon after Mr. William Green was appointed. In the nineteenth century bellmen used to be in great demand, but as Mr. Ben Green told a " Keighley News " reporter on Thurs-

day night, the services of town criers, at any rate in the North of England are rarely needed at the present day. Last year, in fact, Mr. Gr " belled " on only four occasi Three shillings is the usual charge the services of the bellman, but remuneration is generally de the length of the announcem the area in which it is nece this to be read.

Mr. Green intends when to hand the bell over to Mr. Stanley Green carried out the " p crier will ha be four generatio

Joe Green died in 1872 and was succeeded by his son, William, who continued to live in his father's house at 23, Illingworth's Yard, Bingley, which had been the family home for more than 150 years. The original Town Crier's bell was recast soon after William was appointed Town Crier by the Court Leet.

William held the office of Town Crier for more than 60 years. The Yorkshire Post and Intelligencer of 18th August, 1932, includes in its report of The Airedale Show at Bingley the following comment: "*One of the proudest men of the day was Mr William Green, **the bellman**, who was still on duty announcing the classes (of show animals) as he has done at every show in the society's history*". William died less than a year after this event.

Following a period of ill-health late in his life, William expressed the wish that his son Ben, of Crownest Road, Bingley, should carry on the role of Town Crier. William died in 1933 and Ben took over from him as town crier. On succeeding his father, the Telegraph and Argus noted the event in stating: "*Although there is little demand upon the services of any North of England town crier nowadays, the office is still being carried out in Bingley. Mr William Green, who died last week has expressed the wish that his son Mr Ben Green should carry on in his place*".

Sue with the Town Crier's Bell.

Ben himself stated to the Keighley News in 1934 that there was less call for the services of town crier and that "Last year, he had 'belled' on only four occasions. He also observed that *"Three shillings is the usual charge for the services of bellman, but remuneration is generally decided by the length of the announcement and the area where it is necessary to be read".*

Aunt Florrie's Bone of Contention

Sue remembers her Aunt Florrie as a daughter of William Green, being aggrieved that it was only the male line who would be considered for the role of Town Crier. However Sue also recalls that her Aunt didn't want the actual job, only the bell!

While the bell was cleaned and polished during the year it received a special clean by the children of the family at Christmas in anticipation of Aunt Florrie's visit. On her arrival she would demand: "Let me see the bell", and woe betide them if it was not clean and polished!

Long Service to the Town

Ben Green served as town crier for 20 years until he died in 1954. He also identified his son Stanley (Sue's father) as next Town Crier but in the event his services were never called upon. In total the Green family had been town criers for Bingley for just over 100 Years.

BINGLEY TEACHER TRAINING COLLEGE 1926

1911 Main College Building before landscaping of the site.

As part of my Living History approach this chapter looks at the experience of one student, Doris Evelyn Reeve who attended Bingley Teacher Training College between 1926 and 1928. This chapter was the result of several meetings between her daughter, (now Doreen Thompson, who lives in Bingley) and myself in which Doreen recounted her mother's memories of her time at the college. She has also provided me with her Mother's written account of her time there.

In setting the scene, the chapter also gives a background to the period between 1911 and 1926. I also give a background to the siting of the College in Bingley prior to Doris starting there.

1911 - 1916

The formative years of the college were shaped by Helen Wodehouse the first **Principal** of the college who built up the reputation of the institution during its early years including **World War I 1914 - 1918.** This period also saw students and staff contributing to the **war effort.** Students and local schoolchildren also played a part in local pageants celebrating Bingley's history such as the **Masque of the Wool** held in **Myrtle Park** in **1916.**

As Principal, Helen Wodehouse saw that it was **important** that the college was seen to play a part in the **life of Bingley** and so local people were invited to evening lectures and social functions at the college. Additionally, she, colleagues and students took an active part as members of the **Bingley Women's Suffrage Society** which **eventually under her sponsorship became the Women Citizens' League.**

1918 - 1919

An **influenza epidemic** between **June, 1918,** and **May, 1919,** resulted in **260** cases of flu leading to the death of one student from Hild Hall and one from Priestley. At this stage there was **no college sanatorium** (eventually built in 1930) and ill students were nursed in their own halls.

In **July, 1919,** after eight years as Principal of the college, **Dr Wodehouse resigned** to take up a new position at Bristol University as Professor of Education. She was succeeded by **Mary Lilley** who took up her post at the start of the **summer term in 1919** but unfortunately died in December, 1919, at the end of her first term at Bingley.

College Principal Edith Spalding (circled) with junior students.

1920 - 1924

Ethel Spalding was appointed Principal in **1920** and took up her post in **1921**. She became President of the Womens Citizens' League during that year, following on from the community involvement that Helen Wodehouse had previously started. She was Principal of the College until 1933.

In October, **1924,** Bingley as a town held an **Education Week** to bring together the community and the various aspects of local education. The intention of the event seems to have been to showcase local education philosophy and provision to create a better understanding. The college was profiled within the Education Week brochure, as follows: *"The first essential of an educational system is efficient provision for the training of teachers and Bingley is fortunate in having within its borders an up-to-date training college for teachers, though it belongs not to the local system but to the county. The fine buildings consisting of a central block and five residential hostels, were opened in 1911. Their spaciousness and equipment are in marked contrast with the cramped conditions of many still existing training colleges.*

"The normal course is two years, sometimes extended to three. The students, in addition to instruction in the usual academic subjects and in Psychology and Teaching Method, receive much practice in the work for which they are preparing; this is carried out in Bingley schools which are used for demonstration purposes by the college. By this close connection between college and schools the students gain experience of the actual working and everyday difficulties of teaching, while the teachers are able to profit by the inspiration and guidance of the college staff, who also take a leading part in the public work of Bingley, especially that of the League of Nations' Union".

1925 - 1926

In 1925 the quota of places at Bingley College reserved for West Yorkshire students was raised to 50 per cent. This decision was as a direct result of a **general shortage of training college places** throughout the country. This figure was again raised in subsequent years and by 1928,

80 per cent of places at Bingley were reserved for West Yorkshire applicants.

By 1926 college staff and students were active members of both the Womens Citizens' League and the League of Nations' Union. With their counterparts from the Bingley branches of both they organized and held a **joint peace rally in Myrtle Park.**

Student Memories - Doris Reeve
Difficult Times

Doris arrived at the college in 1926. Prior to this she had lived in Barnoldswick with her parents. Her mother worked as a weaver and her father was an office clerk. He encouraged her to sit for a scholarship for Skipton Girls' High School which she passed.

Money was not easily come by and Doris actually made her own blazer for school at the age of ten. After being invalided out of World War I, unfortunately Doris's father died in 1920. Her mother consequently worked 12-hour shifts in the mill as she wanted the best for her daughter.

Undaunted by the circumstances Doris worked in the mill for a summer holiday after which it was decided that she would go back to school. She began doing **work experience** at a local junior school where the head teacher encouraged her to return to her studies and **train to teach**. After gaining her Matriculation she applied to **Bingley College** and was **successful** in gaining a place. She chose music as her main course and art and craft as her secondary course.

A Beautiful Place

After corresponding during the summer holidays with the "senior" student who would mentor her, Doris arrived at Bingley Station in September, 1926. She remembered sharing a taxi with other new recruits and the journey of about a mile up a steep hill to the college. In her own words (and ones that would be echoed by many students over the years) *"My first view of the college far exceeded my expectations, I thought it was a beautiful place".*

Bakehouse (behind the trees) and Hild, Alcuin, Ascham, Priestley and Acland Halls.

Halls of Residence

Doris recalled that "*The five Halls of Residence – Hild, Alcuin, Ascham, Priestley and Acland, were set in a row on terraces. On ground level was a corridor which connected the halls and beneath each hall lived the maids with their own kitchen, dining room, sitting room, bathroom and individual bedrooms.*

All the meals were prepared in the bakehouse (next to the first hall in the row, Hild) and brought along the basement corridor on huge trolleys to be served in each hall".

1927/28 Doris in front of Acland Hall.

A Valley Full of Stars at Night

As a first year Doris was allocated a top floor bedroom in Acland Hall at the back of the hall overlooking fields. Later, as a senior in her second year she was given a ground floor bedroom at the front from which *"you could see the hills across the valley and at night all the lights of Bingley twinkling".*

The college song opening first line, coining a phrase from Helen Wodehouse's inaugural speech captures the muse when it states *"A valley full of stars at night".*

Settling In

New students assisted by senior students soon formed "families" within their halls. Many of these friendships would continue long after they left college.

After the difficult circumstances prior to commencing college, Doris was enraptured with her new life as a student. *"College life was lovely. We had lectures from 9 am to 12.30 pm with breakfast having been at 8 am. Afternoons were free to play games, shop or walk on the moors. Evening lectures started at 4.45 pm and ended at 7.15 pm".*

Meals

Meals seem to have been a feature of the college day. Breakfast consisted of porridge, scrambled or boiled eggs or bacon, marmalade and bread.

After lectures huge plates of parkin squares would be provided in the main college building Common Room at 10.30 am and high tea consisting of bread, butter, jam and cake provided at 4 pm. Lunch (1 pm) and dinner (7.30 pm) were described by Doris as *"sumptuous affairs, where we students on a rota system served lunch and dinner which we collected from a serving hatch in the halls dining room attached to the basement corridor".*

1927/8 Doris (third from left) with friends in the college grounds.

School Teaching Practice

Besides lectures and practicals, students undertook school teaching practice for which they had to prepare their lesson for next day after dinner each night. For Juniors in their **first year** this occurred in **November, 1926,** and **June, 1927.** Doris travelled to Drummond Road Boys School in **Bradford** where she had a class of eight-year-old boys, and thoroughly enjoyed the change. Her second school practice was at Lee's School, Crossroads, near **Keighley**.

During her second year Doris undertook school practice in the **Spring** term of **1928** at Eastwood School, **Keighley**, followed by her **final exams** in which she passed every subject, with a credit in music. She also worked hard on an advanced subject project involving handwork and pottery and successfully designed and made a large foot high coiled pot and a basket chair.

Halls Curator

When senior students left the college, nominations were asked for from the first year juniors for **Halls Officials**, namely Hall President, Secretary, Treasurer and Curator. They worked on the administration and organising of each Hall with the Warden a resident member of staff . Doris became Curator unopposed and gained a front of the building bedroom where she "now had a lovely view", in a room next door to the Halls Warden.

Her duties included making the rotas for serving at table, collecting and taking letters to post, sitting at high table with the warden, making sure that entrance "ends" were tidy and booking meals for visitors to hall.

Social Activities

Doris also thoroughly enjoyed the variety of activities and societies at the college which seems to have provided opportunities to work hard and play hard.

She had a love of the **outdoors**, which her daughter, Doreen, would later inherit and was an active member of the Rambling Society held on Saturdays. There were many **walks across the moors** from the college and successive generations of students would call these the "fifteen" "thirty", "sixty" and "ninety", so called after the time it took to complete them.

Other activities included a musical society, a dancing society, country dancing and outside lectures by notable personalities of the day. Dances were held in the college hall and staff also provided a "Staff Impromptu" which usually depicted scenes from college life including humorous digs at students or outside lecturers.

1927/28 Doris in college blazer on the moors near the college.

Students also presented their own Impromptu held on Saturdays, when each hall would draw a topic from either Grand Opera, Pantomime, Variety, Drama or Musical Comedy. They then had the rest of the day to rehearse their theme and prepare costumes.

A Career in Teaching

On leaving the college, Doris gained valuable experience as a supply teacher in Barnoldswick and even had two months as a head teacher in a two-teacher rural school. She gained her first full-time teaching post with a class of 57 children in November, 1929, at the Church of England School that she herself had attended.

She never forgot her time at the college or the **friends** that she had made there. During her career she taught and lived in Barnoldswick, Earby, Selby and Goole. She passed away in November, 1992, and is fondly remembered by her family.

500 YEARS IN THE BINGLEY AREA

Stuart Clark with the family tree he commissioned through genealogy research.

This chapter relates to one family living in Bingley over a period of nearly 500 years. It is the result of several meetings with local man Stuart Clark who in 2011 decided to find out more about his ancestors. Stuart gave me full access to the records he has collected relating to his family.

Voyage of Discovery

During the meetings I asked asked Stuart to describe how he went about his "voyage of discovery" and why. The second part of this chapter explores why and how he did so and is intended to help readers wishing to do the same have a useful template with which to start their own 'voyage'.

500 Years in the Bingley Area

Stuart, of Lane End Farm, Gilstead, describes himself as "*a Bingley man born and bred*". His interest in the local history of his family led him to contract with a genealogist to research his family back to the earliest possible date.

This turned out to be a journey of nearly 500 years with Stuart finding evidence that during the 1500s and 1600s there were a number of Clerke families living in of Bingley. Anthonie Clerke of Priestthorpe, William Clerke of Beckfoot, and Edmund Clerke of Bingley are the main identified heads of family during this time.

Definitive Dates

Records show that the earliest definite links to Stuart start with John Clerke, born in 1651/1652, the son of either Edmund (1616) or William Clerke (1621). By 1677 the medieval spelling of Clerke had changed to Clark (also sometimes shown with an e as in Clarke). Records then show the existence of the Clark family in Bingley linking Stuart to Jonathan Clark (1696), John Clark (1720), Jonathan Clark (1743), John Clark (1749), William Clark (1756), Jonathan Clark (1784), William Clark (1811), Thomas Clark (1846) Percy Clark (1885) and Frank Clark 1924) who was Stuart's father.

Working as Stonemasons

The male side of the Clark family have long been recorded working mainly as stonemasons living in the local area. There is also a record in the 1871 Census of Ann Clark (nee Raistrick)) the widow of William Clark which shows her as a stone quarry occupier living at Langley, Bingley. Her son Jonathan was a Stone Miner and another son, Thomas (Stuart's great grandfather) is shown as being a stone mason. Thomas would later play a prominent part in the formation of the present pack of Airedale Beagles and would become their first Huntsman, a post he held from 1891 until his retirement in 1900.

According to Stuart, his Aunt, Winifred Clark, married into the family of John Holdsworth Clark and Son (no relation) who were the principal

Tom Clark - Huntsman of Airedale Beagles.

masons in the early 1920s involved in carving the cenotaph in Myrtle Park to commemorate the World War I dead of Bingley.

How Far Did they Move?

Genealogy records show that the main areas/addresses for Stuart's relations have been in the Bingley, Gilstead and Eldwick areas, namely: Priestthorpe, Dubb Lane, Carrier Row (off Chapel Lane), Adelaide Street, Langley, Park View, Crow Nest, Ferncliffe Road and Fernbank Drive. In essence this means that the family have lived in an area within a **radius of approximately one mile** in the Bingley area for several hundred years.

Family Size

Up to the mid 1800s the Clark family are recorded as having four generations with a **family size** of eight, one of eleven, one of seven and one of four. Between the 1600s and 1800 there are eight recorded **infant deaths** within the family, two in each generation. The majority of baptisms and records of burials for the family were at **Bingley Parish Church**.

Sources of Information

In 2011 after contacting **Bradford Registry Office** to ask for advice, Stuart identified a genealogist and contracted him to *"Research as far back as you can – What are my family connections to Bingley?"* At this stage, through local sources Stuart had knowledge of his family going back 150 years, but not beyond.

He and the genealogist met every two weeks over a period of a year and Stuart professes to being amazed by the amount of detail revealed. He paid as he went along to cover costs for records including **birth, marriage** and **death** certificates and time-consuming searches of **Church records** and **graves in Bingley Cemetery**. The researcher also checked records in other local towns particularly for **marriage links**. Details of occupations for the Clark family were accessed through **Census Records** and several **online sources** advised on by **Bradford Libraries Local Studies**.

Value for Money?

As a result of the research Stuart has built up a catalogue of four folders covering the history of his family, plus a **detailed family tree**. He has been surprised by the depth of information, his only regret being that there were very few photographs kept by his predecessors. He regards the money spent on the research as *"the best money spent in my life"*.

Links to the Past

What Stuart feels is that the information generated has given him a real sense of the lives his ancestors must have led. He says: *"I feel that I can picture and walk in the footsteps they walked as I now have a better understanding of the poverty, tragedy, good and bad times they went through, that I can compare to modern times and my own life. I also have a real sense of how as ordinary Bingley people they adapted to difficult times and looked after each other.*

Now has been the right stage in my life to seek to find out more about my family, before it is too late in terms of my own time clock. I'd like this chapter to be a testament to the Clark family and to dedicate it to my father, Frank, and my mother, Beryl Hermione Clark, who died in 2013".

VISITING MY FATHER'S BIRTHPLACE - BINGLEY

Michael Wilde, who now lives with his family in Los Osos, California, recounts a visit that they made to Bingley in May, 2013. Michael's grandfather, Joseph, emigrated to America from Bingley in 1907 and Michael has been carrying out research into his Bingley roots from a distance. Here he describes the reasons for the visit and what he discovered.

When planning a three-month European travel adventure for our family, a visit to Bingley, Yorkshire, England was top of our list. On top of the list **because** *my father Geoffrey (B. Wild) Wilde was born in Bingley on April 20, 1901, at 36, Knight Street.*

It was time to share my heritage with my wife and twin daughters. They wanted to know, **"Are we related to Robin Hood or King Arthur?"**

Local History

In making arrangements for a week's stay at the Five Rise Locks Hotel, I asked the owner, Richard Stoyle, if he could suggest a local historian. He put me in contact with Alan Cattell, local historian and author, who graciously gave us walking and driving tours of Bingley and district during our visit in May, 2013.

Alan met us at the Five Rise Locks Hotel and took us out for a walk from Beck Lane up to **Gawthorpe Hall**, *where our Wild/Wilde family research has come to a dead end with the birth in about 1650 of Nicholas Wilde and his marriage to Frances Greene on 28 October 1677 in* **Bingley Parish Church**.

We walked along many of the place names I had only read about in census records and on old maps – **Crownest, Priestthorpe, Leeds & Liverpool Canal.**

Geneology Research

Since the 1970s, I have been involved in **genealogy research about my Bingley family,** *when I developed a Wilde Family Recipe Collection publishing project to capture stories and favourite recipes from my English*

The Joseph Wild Family in 1907 at Bingley, Yorkshire, England: Standing, from left, Geoffrey, Louis Frederick, William Ernest, Lena, Edgar, Edith, Arthur, Sydney Hanson. Seated, from left, Janet, Joseph Wild and Clara Elstub Wild.

191

relatives to share with my extended family. Susan McPherson Wilde, wife of my cousin, Gordon Wilde, joined me in my research in the 1990s. She jumped into all the details as the genealogy research world was moving from microfiche to the Internet. She made numerous contacts via the **Yorkshire Archives** *list service, along with extensive research using the* **Latter Day Saints** *archives. I have continued the research, enhancing the detailed history that started to emerge of my* **ancestors – farmers, stonemasons, and worsted weavers.**

From Bingley to America

My grandfather **Joseph Wild** *and his wife* **Clara Elstub Wild** *left Bingley in July, 1907, sailing for America with all nine children. They settled first in Rhode Island, and then drove west to California in 1920. Earlier, my great uncle Harry Wild, son of William Wild, and his wife Bessie Taylor Wood had sailed for America, also settling in* **New England***. On applying for naturalization, my grandfather decided to add an 'e' on the end of his name to differentiate his family from the Harry Wild's. To make Wild/Wilde matters even more confusing, two of Harry's daughters married two of Joseph's sons after moving to America!*

Bingley Relatives

Through research, a number of Bingley relatives have become apparent, including **William Wild,** *one of the* **stone masons who constructed the Five Rise Locks** *(1774),* **Lily Elstub,** *publican of the* **Old Queens Head** *(1930s),* **David Hanson,** *one of the founders (1853) of the* **Bingley Industrial Cooperative Society,** *and* **Mary Gott Wild***), publican of the* **Royal Oak** *(1845-1853).*

A Warm Welcome and Hospitality

While in Bingley, I scooped up as many locally published books on Bingley as I could, including Alan Cattell's latest Bingley and Surrounds, Forgotten Moments from History, and mailed them home. My family and I walked the gravestones at the **Parish Church** *and the paths of the* **Bingley Cemetery***. While on the towpath at the Five Rise Locks we were invited by a couple to*

Michael Wilde and Alan in 2013.

go aboard their canal boat and ride several lock changes. I could see the stones my relative **William Wild had placed with his own hands.** *A hailstorm forced us to make a run for the Five Rise Locks Café where we enjoyed a delicious lunch in the* **former canal horse stables.**

Finally, walking **Old Main Street,** *stopping at shops on Main Street, enjoying the wonderful hospitality of the Five Rise Locks Hotel, Loft Café, Cardamon Restaurant and celebrating our anniversary at Valentino Ristorante, we* **came away from Bingley feeling very much at home.** *Thank you to everyone who made our stay so special and helped my family see our English origins come alive.*

BARRY WATSON - BINGLEY'S WORLD RECORD CHANNEL SWIMMER

This chapter is based on my interviews with Barry Watson from Crossflatts, who in 1964 became a World Record holding Channel Swimmer.

The chapter is intended to identify the events leading up to and subsequent to such a major achievement and some of the many key people who influenced and helped Barry along the way.

Early Days, Primary School and Ill Health

Barry Watson was born in Shipley in 1938, the son of a butcher. At an early age he went to live with his grandfather in Crownest Road, Bingley, and attended Belgrave Road and Mornington Road schools. In his youth Barry contracted double pneumonia and was not expected to live through the experience and later, measles, which badly affected his eyesight.

Despite these drawbacks he had a key advantage, a grandfather who became his motivator and mentor and who encouraged him to use a chest expander to exercise and build up his strength. Still in Barry's possession is a silver cup which his grandfather won in 1907 when competing in a 40 yards swimming championship at Shipley Baths. This stimulated Barry's early interest in swimming.

Secondary School

In 1949, Barry went to the Modern School, Bingley (now Beckfoot) and was introduced to swimming by Johnny Rock who played Rugby League for Keighley. In his second year at the school his teacher Margaret Wilman, also took an interest. There was a 'house' system at the school with the four 'houses' being Gawthorpe, Ryshworth, Milner and St Ives (all named after notable mansion houses in the Bingley area). Barry was in Gawthorpe House.

He remembers that initially swimming consisted of playing 'tig' in Bingley Baths. While in the second year he progressed to competing in the 75 yards sprint (three lengths of the pool) and became School Champion, competing and winning against boys older than himself. He recalls that he won the Championship three years in a row.

Barry, his sisters and a training partner, Selwyn Hird, – midwinter in the River Aire.

Technical School and Apprenticeship

In years three and four at the Modern School, Barry and Harvey Smith, a friend from his first two years, commenced studying building in the technical part of the school. After leaving school in 1953 Barry became an apprentice compositor in the printing industry.

Both Barry and Harvey would eventually become internationally recognised, Harvey as a show jumper and Barry as a long distance open water swimmer.

While serving his apprenticeship, Barry continued to train at various indoor swimming pools namely Bingley, Keighley, Shipley Old Pool and Le Page Street Bradford, building up the length of the distances he swam. Additionally he began to use the outdoor pools at Bradford Lido (now Lister Park) and at Otley to build up his ability to swim longer distances as a precursor to open water swims.

First Open Water Swim

At the age of 18 Barry competed in his first serious open water swim, the one mile Clyde-Firth swim. Here he learned an important lesson as regards being slow into the water when the starter's gun went off. This never happened again and in future years several of Barry's coaches would comment that he had a good style, but swam too fast in terms of endurance swimming!

National Service

Between 1960 and 1962 Barry served his National Service at Chilwell in Nottinghamshire but during his service he did little or no swimming and for two years did not train.

Training Resumes!

On leaving the Services he resumed his training with Geoff Oddie as his trainer. Additional help was given by Bert Lax, the manager at Bingley Pool who gave Barry a key to the baths so that he could carry out training in the early morning and after work. In the two years leading up to his first Channel swim Barry became the British Long

Distance Swimming Association Champion at Lake Windermere in 1963 and 1964 and the 16-mile Fleetwood to Morecambe Champion in 1963.

First Channel Swim 1964

By August, 1964, Barry was ready for his first attempt at swimming the Channel hoping to beat the British Record of 12 hours 30 minutes. August is generally the month when conditions are good and most swims are attempted. The date he started his attempt was the 16th of August and he set off from France at 2 am, the tides dictating the best time for swims to be started. Barry remembers the hotel manager giving up his own bed at the Cap Gris Nez Hotel so that Barry could rest prior to the attempt. He also recalls being given a meal of chicken and chips an hour prior to the swim to keep his strength up!

Sponsorship

Seven other swimmers set off at the same time in choppy conditions and Barry was supported by his coach, Geoff Oddie, who accompanied him in a trawler. Prior to the swim Watmough's Printers, Barry's then employers, had donated £100 towards his attempt and through public subscriptions and fund raising events he had raised £300 towards accommodation, transport and trawler costs (of £75).

PRINCESS HALL BATHS - BINGLEY

WAT**S**ON
SUPER**S**WIM**S**HOW

High Board Capers
Monte Christo Sack Dive
Long & Short Squadron Race
School Childrens Events
Anne's Tadpoles
Surprise Item

PERSONAL APPEARANCE OF
CHANNEL SWIMMERS AND LOCAL CHAMPIONS

JULY 15th 1964
7-30 p.m.
UNDER A.S.A. LAWS

IN AID OF BARRY WATSONS' CHANNEL SWIM FUND
Tickets Available at Princess Hall Baths

Adults 2/-   **Children 1/-**

Barry acknowledges that as an amateur, while he did not make any money, he was lucky enough to receive sponsorship from a number of sources. Fields Printers of Lidgett Green, Bradford, a future sponsor and employer of Barry's, also assisted his long distance swimming career.

A World Record!

Barry covered the 22 mile-swim from France in a World Record 9 hours and 35 minutes, reaching St Margaret's Bay, Dover, at 11.35 am on the Sunday morning. He remembers that initially few people were there to cheer him ashore because in planning a swim, due to the tides, no-one knows definitely where they are going to land. Barry's time beat the existing World Record France to England swim by an hour, a record which would stand for a further 18 years.

Barrys Certificate from the Channel SwimmingAssociation recognising his World Record Time of 1964.

A Good Weekend for Yorkshire

Just prior to Barry's record another had been set by Fred Trueman, the Yorkshire and England cricketer. Fred became the first bowler to take 300 Test wickets in a career, which he achieved while playing at the Oval in the Fifth Test against Australia. Trueman then travelled to Dover where Yorkshire were playing Kent. Sensing an important occasion, the Press organised a presentation at the White Cliffs Hotel, Dover to which they invited Fred and Barry to celebrate their achievements.

Barry remembers Trueman jokingly remarking to him that it had taken him 'years' to set his record, whereas Barry had become famous in only 9 hours 35 minutes! Barry replied that what Trueman hadn't taken into account was the many hours that he had spent in isolated training.

Both men kept in contact with each other until Fred Trueman died in 2006.

Presentation in Bingley

At the end of August, 1964, a civic reception was held at Bingley Town Hall at Myrtle Park after a motorcade procession attended by thousands of Bingley residents. Barry still has in his possession a film of the celebration at which he was presented with a silver salver from the people of Bingley.

Further Long Distance Championships

During a busy period in the 1960s Barry became champion at the following events:

1964: Windermere

1965: Fleetwood to Morecambe

1966: 2 Way - Windermere and Fleetwood to Morecambe

1967: Fleetwood to Morecombe, Loch Lomond and 2 Way - Windermere

1968: 2 Way - Windermere

He is particulary proud of two swims where he set new records, namely the Fleetwood to Morecambe 16 miles which he covered in 4 hours 7 minutes and the Lancaster to Morecambe 23 miles which took him 7 hours 2 minutes.

He would go on to swim Windermere 39 times and Coniston 47 times as well as on one occasion swimming Windermere, Coniston and Ullswater all in the same day.

Further Channel Swims

During 1968, 1969 and 1970 Barry again swam the Channel but as two-way attempts on each occasion. Unfortunately, bad weather conditions forced him to abandon the two-way attempts. His times of 15 hours and 21 minutes, 13 hours and 56 minutes and 15 hours and 14 minutes still represent a significant achievement when you consider that Barry was a full-time employee and an amateur swimmer!

International Recognition

In 1972 the International Swimming Hall of Fame in Florida USA recognised the scale of Barry's swimming exploits by inducting him as an Honour Swimmer.

Enjoying the Outdoors

Overcoming the ill-health of his early youth, Barry proved that hard work, dedication and training using local facilities and mentors and coaches could reap international recognition and rewards.

He is still an active fell walker having completed all 214 of the Wainwright fell walks in the Lake District and a total of 77 of Munros in Scotland (mountains above 3,000 feet).

While still a swimmer, his interests nowadays revolve around following fell running and athletics. He closely follows the exploits of his friend Ian Holmes a British Fell Running Champion (Three Peaks, Snowden and Ben Nevis winner). Barry is also a close friend of Chris Cariss of Bingley Harriers who ran the London Marathon in 2004 with a fractured heel in a time of 2 hours 15 minutes and 8 Seconds.

Barry in 2013 holding his grandfather's 1907 swimming trophy with the Brownlee Brothers competing in the background – heroes across the years!

Perhaps Barry's greatest current passion and interest is in the Triathlon which combines his interest in swimming and running with cycling. On Tuesday evenings most weeks he can be found watching his friends Alastair and Jonathan Brownlee training at Leeds Metropolitan University Campus.

One of Life's Enthusiasts!

Meeting Barry you soon realise that you are in the presence of a knowledgeable sporting enthusiast who enjoys a good natter about the sporting exploits of others rather than himself. I found that the admiration that he had for his grandfather's sporting achievement and support and his avid interest and excitement in the progress of the Brownlee Brothers and other athletes are a testament to this self-effacing mans approach to life.

2016 - A Sequel

Since I interviewed Barry in 2013 I've met up with him on a number of occasions. Certainly, 2016 has been a good year for him as his friends, the Brownlees, achieved gold and silver medals in the Rio Olympics. He still watches them training at the track on a Tuesday night and at the pool on Wednesdays. In keeping his hand in Barry says": *I suppose it's because I enjoy going to the swim sessions and Jonny nearly always asks me what I think about his technique*".

He certainly seems to get out what he puts into life in terms of his continuing energy and comes across as someone who is very content with his lot.

A Fitting End

In considering a fitting end to this book it seemed obvious to me that Barry might be a perfect person to summarise what Bingley means to him and to others who have lived here for a long time.

So here are his thoughts and words in representing *Bingley – A Living History:* "*I've lived in Bingley all my 78 years, 54 of them in my present house. I've always been very happy here.*

There have been changes, not always for the best, but there have also been improvements. You have to weigh one up against the other. Taking everything into consideration it's a great place to live and I wouldn't want to be anywhere else".

BIBLIOGRAPHY AND REFERENCES

Bibliography

Baldwin. H. (*2005*) *Images of England: Bingley Revisited*

Barnwell. P.S. and Giles. C. (1997) *English Farmsteads 1750 – 1914*

Cattell. A. (*2011*) *Bingley and Surrounds – Forgotten Moments from History*

Clarke (*2011*) *A Rapid Assessment of Four Historic Farmsteads on the Drummond Estate – Lubberthorpe , Leicestershire*

Crawford. E. (*1999*) *The Women's Suffrage Movement – A Reference Guide 1866-1928*

Cudworth. W. (*1876*) *Round About Bradford*

Downsborough. E. (*2009*) *The Lost Pubs of Bingley – From the Old Coaching Inns to The Humble Beerhouses*

Downsborough. E. (*2011*) *Bingley's Historic Pubs*

Dodd. E.E. (*1958*) *Bingley*

Gregory. J. (*2005*) *Fred Hoyle's Universe*

Harrison. W. (*1997*) *Day's Awake – Childhood Memories of Bingley*

Hartley (*1900*) *50 Years of Cooperation in Bingley : A Jubilee Record of the Bingley Industrial Cooperative Society, Ltd*

Healey. E. (**1885**) *A Series of Picturesque Views and Country Houses in Yorkshire*

Horsfall Turner (*1897*) *Ancient Bingley: Or Bingley, Its History and Scenery*

Hoyle. F. (*1986*) *The Small World of Fred Hoyle*

Hoyle. F. (*1968*) *Encounter with The Future.* Simon and Schuster

Hoyle. F. (*1994*) *Home is Where the Wind Blows – Chapters from a Cosmologists Life*

Mitton. S. (*2005*) *Fred Hoyle, A Life In Science – Conflict in the Cosmos.*

Snow. J. (*2009*) *Bingley's Fabulous Fifties Featuring the Basement Girls*

Speight. H. (*1898*) *Chronicles and Stories of Old Bingley*

Van den Dael. R. and Davide Beal. R. (2011) *Milner Field –The Lost Country House of Titus Salt Jr*

Varo. S. (*1985*) *Shipley Glen Ride*

Wade-Martins. S. *The English Model Farm : Building the Architectural Ideal 1700 – 1914*

White. W. (*1837*) *History, Gazetteer and Directory of the West Riding of Yorkshire. Volume 1*

Winchester. C. (Ed) (*1933*) *The World Film Encyclopedia*

Newspapers

Bingley Chronicle *January 31st, 1908, March 19th, 1909*

Bradford Observer *December 1861, September 5th, 1874*

Derby Daily Telegraph *February 14th, 1907*

Evening Post *April, 1901, April, 1907*

Jersey Evening Post *May, 1924*

Keighley Herald *February 22nd, 1907*

Keighley News *September 3rd, 1904, June 5th, 1905, July 19th, 1907, October 7th, 1911, July 2nd, 1917, 1934*

Leeds Mercury *April 20th, 1872, October 12th, 1872, January 19th, 1880, January 24th, 1880, February 22nd, 1887, March 12th, 1892, June 26th, 1899*

The Times *July 3rd, 1936*

Votes for Women *June 18th, 1908, August 27th, 1908*

York Herald *May 12th, 1883, August 26th, 1899, August 31st, 1883*

Yorkshire Evening Post *August 6th, 1901, January 28th, 1926, September 23rd, 1926*

Yorkshire Post and Leeds Intelligencer *August 10th, 1901, March 20th, 1922, April 11th, 1922, August, 1932*

Magazines and Journals

Bingley College Magazine, *1965*

Building News *December 22nd, 1876*

Gardeners Magazine *November 23rd, 1889*

Hannam J (2011) Women of the Right Spirit - Paid Organizers of the Women's Social and Political Movement (WSPU) *1904-1918 Women's History Series Journal. Volume 20-2011 Issue 1*

Public Papers

Clarke. S. (*2011*) Historic Buildings Assessment - Historic Farmsteads at New Lubberstone. University of Leicestershire

Haigh. S. (*2002*) The Old Fire Station, Market Street, Bingley. Architectural Building Recording for Historic England

Milner Field Indenture Papers *1869* West Yorkshire Archives

Parliamentary Briefing Paper *May, 2015* - Parish and Town Council Powers

The Theatre Trust 1974 accessed on *July 5th, 2016* at: www. theatrestrust.org.uk/resources/theatres/show/2402-bingley-arts-centre-home-of-bingley-little-theatre.

Wooler. F. (*2015*) Milner Field Innovation Centre, Milner Field Farm, Gilstead- Archeology and Cultural Assessment. Wardell Armstrong

Brochure

Bingley Education Week Brochure October 1924. Available Bradford Libraries Local Studies

Online Sources

www.hoyle.org.uk
www.joh.cam.uk.ac.uk/Library

INDEX